ERIC
A YOUNG TEENAGE
KENTUCKY BOY

STRUGGLES ALONG HIS ROAD
OF CHRISTIAN SERVICE

ERIC
A YOUNG TEENAGE
KENTUCKY BOY

STRUGGLES ALONG HIS ROAD
OF CHRISTIAN SERVICE

WINSTON OSBORNE

XULON PRESS

Xulon Press
2301 Lucien Way #415
Maitland, FL 32751
407.339.4217
www.xulonpress.com

Unless otherwise indicated, Scripture quotations taken
from the Holy Bible, New International Version (NIV).
Copyright © 1973, 1978, 1984, 2011 by Biblica, Inc.™.
Used by permission. All rights reserved.

Scripture quotations taken from the King James Version
(KJV)–*public domain*.

Printed in the United States of America.

ISBN-13: 978-1-54565-991-5

A LIST OF CHARACTERS

Eric Bray: son of Elbert and Mabel Bray

Tom Bray: Eric's brother

Julie Bray: Eric's sister

Uncle Esau: Eric's Great Uncle

Ron Milford: son of John and Ethel

Larry: Ron's brother

Mr. Hunley: Eric's preacher

Willard and Maratha Asberry: Eric's neighbors

Eugene West: Eric's relative

Mr. Walker: Eric's sixth-grade teacher

Jr. Brooks: Bus driver and Arlene, his wife

Coy: A deacon who drove a tractor and gave Eric a thumbs up

Mrs. Wilson and Mrs. Smith: Eric's seventh-grade teachers

Ms. Anderson and Mr. Ray: Eric's eighth-grade teachers

Mr. Bob, Mr. Gene, and Ms. Samantha: high school teachers

Mr. Halbright: Eric's principal (7-12)

Darla Aby: Girlfriend

Alford and Albert: ninth grade classmates

Mike Coffee: Tried to trip Eric and ended up with a limp

Ellen, Arthur, Allen, and George: Involved with making shine

Ellis Duke and Rocky Ford: Eric's friends in Illinois

Hobert: Drunk truck driver

NOTES

1. The Scriptures quoted or referenced in this book are taken from the Holy Bible, New International Version (NIV), Copyright 1973, 1978, 1984, 2011 by Biblica, Inc. Used by permission of Zondervan. Or taken from the Kings James Version (KJV), public domain.

2. The song, "I Am Thine O Lord" written by Fanny J. Crosby is public domain.

3. The author composed the entire content of this book.

4. Names, places, and incidents in this composition are used fictitiously or are of the author's imagination.

5. I began writing this narrative in 2010. One of my objectives was to show a contrast between preteens' life today, to life in the forties and early fifties.

6. Another goal was, I inserted a little humor along with some serious reflections of what

life is all about. I've tried to explain many of my actual lifetime experiences, truthful and imaginary thoughts I had while growing up. I described the experiences realistically, then added a little humor to appeal to the intended reader.

TABLE OF CONTENTS

PREFACE

THIS NARRATIVE ILLUSTRATES THE HARM done to Eric, a young Kentucky boy with a language limitation. When he was five, a doctor diagnosed him as having Ankyloglossia (also known as tongue-tie), a mild case of tongue manipulation. The doctor informed his parents that an operation might improve his pronunciation, but with age and effort, he thought Eric could overcome this problem. However, the doctor felt the procedure was too experimental, so Eric's parents decided against it.

Young Eric was considered shy and bashful. He coped with insinuations and laughter during his youth. Some were intentional, others jokingly, or others were woven into group dialogue. The most hurtful ones came from adults. These frequent or atypical occurrences built from early childhood left a permanent reservoir for future mental and physical behavior. How he handled these implications affected the way he reasoned, his intuitive understanding of adults, and the discernment of conversations. It is difficult to conclude how children will react or how long the hurt will last. For Eric, it continued far beyond his teenage years; the hurt still stung when adults tittered at a floundered attempt of his articulation of individual words. When this occurred, Eric, as a teenager or a young adult, used the same childlike response to soothe the sting; some of the pain was self-inflicted. His self-esteem dangled like a broken twig ready to fall to the ground; it hung precariously for years. Eric's family and the guidance of the Holy Spirit caught the twig before it fell. After Eric accepted Jesus Christ at the age of thirteen, the Holy Spirit worked years to anchor the process of relieving anger, resentment, and bitterness; this resulted in Eric understanding how to forgive and let go. Follow him through his happiness, sadness, adventures, friendships, and troublesome times along his road of Christian service.

One must never underestimate the overall ability of anyone regardless of age or his confines. We form opinions on each verbal or bodily dialogue. The painful lessons he learned as a youngster followed him beyond his teenage years. Comprehensive knowledge of one area—such as nature, science, books, or sports—will anchor good self-esteem if thoughtless adults do not derail it. This self-assured source will blossom and expand into another aplomb. One may not respond verbally, but children interpret all forms of communication, and few are inscrutable.

As a youngster, Eric listened and learned from life experiences whether amid conversations or in God's natural world. As you read the pages of this book, those youthful lessons are still a valuable part of his psychological makeup as a teenager and young adult. A young man tells this narrative through his eyes while managing life experiences as a young Christian. When hurt turned into anger, and anger became resentment, and resentment developed into a grudge, the Holy Spirit warned him of the dangers to his walk with the Lord.

Eric found no lengthy camaraderie among local youth, so he developed a close friendship with Ron, a boy his age. The family moved from Northern Kentucky into the neighborhood when Eric finished the sixth grade. Eric was skeptical of Ron's family at first, but as the two preteens shared time exploring the palisades of a small creek, known as Barney's Branch, they became close friends. During the seventh grade, Eugene West became an enthusiastic friend in the short episodes of the open countryside.

Christian nurturing enabled Eric to believe in and accept Jesus Christ as his Savior; he was baptized when he was thirteen years old—a correct preparatory stance for a successful teen and adult development.

The desire and purpose of this narrative are to give true childish backgrounds of thoughts, behavior, rationale, logic, and reasoning that lasted during his maturing adult years. This account describes a young adult struggling to manage what he considered hurts and how Christ influenced the outcome.

Envision yourself being in the country in the late forties and fifties; there were no shopping malls, no fast-food restaurants, no bought toys, a pieced-together bicycle—only farm work, church, and school attendance, and three buddies with whom to camp and explore the surrounding woodlands and caves.

CHAPTER 1

ERIC'S HOME LIFE

ERIC BRAY LIVED WITH HIS PARENTS ON a rural farm far from the Pulaski County seat of Somerset, Kentucky. In addition to his parents, Elbert and Mabel, Eric's siblings were a brother, Tom and a sister, Julie.

Agricultural products were the only source of family income. Occasionally, Eric earned four to five dollars per day doing rigorous work for neighbors. He used this money to buy clothing, shoes, and school supplies.

The families in this close-knit community regularly attended the small local church. Revivals drew families from miles away, strengthening friendships. During many summer revivals, his church overflowed, and people stood outside near open windows to hear the message. The church leadership also organized many community activities. "Love thy neighbor" was their motto. The leaders planned road repair, grave diggings, and special holiday get-togethers.

A well-known neighbor delivered weekday mail from the nearby town of Eubank. The "mailman" personally knew the families on his long rural route of rough gravel roads. The "mailman" was a connection to the outside world. When the mail arrived, as a young boy, Eric raced down the one-fourth mile private lane to retrieve it for his parents. Often, he sat impatiently waiting under an apple tree in the orchard wondering what the "mailman" would bring. Would it be an unexpected package, letter, another new Sears Roebuck catalog, or Bible tracts for Dad?

Another well-known neighbor ran a "huckster route." The flatbed truck pulled into the driveway, parked, then lowered steps that allowed the potential shopper access to a small array of groceries. The walk-in storage compartment shelves had non-perishables like salt, sugar, pepper, Kool-Aid, a few canned vegetables, a choice of hard candies, bar hand soap, detergents, chewing tobacco, cigarettes, snuff, and occasionally in-season fresh fruit. The route originated from Todd Store, two miles away and traveled miles around the countryside offering "staples" from the back of his truck. A dense layer of fine limestone dust settled on all merchandise as it floated up through the crevices of the flat wooden truck bed. Instead of money, the value of fresh eggs or heavy cream often paid for the necessities. At the end of each long route, the truck returned to the store to reload for the following day.

There was no television in Eric's home. Television programming was available only by a roof antenna for neighbors who could afford the service. However, storms or heavy clouds either blocked or caused poor reception.

His father listened to the radio in the early mornings, during lunch and late evenings. It was a commodity guarded closely in its use. Eric's father considered this appliance fragile and allowed no one to use it except himself or Eric's mother. Local and state news kept the household informed of weather conditions, deaths, political events, and a few admired ministers. Sunday morning gospel singing echoed throughout the family home with humming from the kitchen adding to the discourse. The palpable Sunday mornings added to the hustle and bustle of doing chores, readying for church attendance and the anticipation of visiting a beloved neighbor.

Eric's sister enjoyed using the costly multiple party-line telephone system. Telephone communication ran over low hanging metal lines on poles found along the roadway. Many households had no telephone. Eric had no interest in using the phone or learning how voices traveled over metal wire lines. Many times, neighbors listened to other people's conversations. Everyone knew to avoid "nosey meddlers" in all personal disclosures. One nosey person in Eric's view tried to dress to suggest that she was opulent. Eric reserved his verbal opinion about these iconic community "nosey meddlers."

In the spring of 1949, Eric's father desired to build a new home on the same site as the old house. To accomplish this, the living and dining rooms of the old home were torn down, leaving only the kitchen for preparation of meals. The family moved to the loft of the nearby woodhouse. The loft had a window on each end covered with transparent plastic for sunlight; the wide open cracks in the oak wood siding provided fresh air circulation. Cardboard covered the widest cracks, preventing wind from blowing water through and soaking the bedding. It was an exciting time for an eight-year-old adventurous Kentucky boy who had an enormous imagination sharpened by his uncle Esau's fascinating tales of life on an Oregon sheep ranch.

Uncle Esau was Eric's great-uncle, and when the doctor removed the leg below the knee, Uncle Esau moved in with Eric's grandparents. He sat in a wheelchair and drifted off to sleep most of the day. Eric assisted his grandfather in caring for his uncle for two months before Uncle Esau passed away. After rolling him in his wheelchair to the back porch, Eric would sit and listen to tales of wild mountainous experiences. Uncle Esau passed away in April of

1954, leaving a void in Eric's life but a bunch of treasured memories.

The new house replacing the old home had a long front concrete porch that stretched the entire width of the house. The sassafras wooden porch swing was saved and hung from the ceiling on the new porch. Few neighbors had porch swings so visitors, especially the young, coveted it. Two cane-laced rocking chairs sat next to it, usually reserved for older folks. Several chairs in poor repair occupied the other side. When neighbors came to visit, the two-foot high concrete porch edge became seating for children and adults. It was an excellent place to sit to enjoy a cold piece of watermelon just taken from overnight cooling in the thirty-five-foot deep well. Several homemade wind chimes hanging from the ceiling played music. This new house had running water, a living room, three small bedrooms, a full dining room, a kitchen, a full basement, a back porch, and the upstairs where Eric and brother Tom slept. This house was well-built by using solid oak timbers cut from the Bray's woods, and no snow penetrated the roof. During a cold wintry night, they sank deep in a feather bed with several layers of homemade quilts on top. The only visible sign of each person was just part of the head needed to breathe. As Eric lay under this new roof on cold nights, he remembered the wood shingled-covered old house that allowed fine-blowing snow to penetrate through the roof leaving a thin layer of snow on the thick quilted bed. Now, in the well-roofed home, they dressed hurriedly and rushed downstairs to the warm modern coal stove. Eric's mother always kindled the morning fire from the wood that he or Tom had piled high in the wood box the night before. Wood started the fire; then coal was piled on the logs for long-lasting heat.

The Brays bought an electric stove and positioned it on the other side of the room, leaving the old cast iron stove for canning vegetables during the summer and heat during the winter. The massive cast iron cooking stove took up most of the space in the kitchen. The sizeable wood-heated stove afforded cooking space for several pots. Two feet above the cooking surface, an enclosed storage compartment kept bread fresh until the next meal. Water carried from the well and placed in a reservoir next to the firebox heated while the other side of the stove supplied ample storage for cooking utensils. Water heated in a teakettle gave another source of needed hot water. Just inside the dining room, a "punched tin" pie safe stored clean bowls, plates, cups, glasses, and condiments. The unique metal door panels had a series of small holes to ventilate the safe. Many in the community thought the white "pie safe" unique because of solid wood construction and the oddly shaped doors.

In 1950, the Brays were able to buy a Hotpoint refrigerator for the new house. Eric, Tom, and Julie were delighted to see that big white box sitting in the corner of the dining room; the food sat just across the room. No need to store food in the chilly water of a nearby spring to keep it from spoiling; no need for three trips each day to bring food from the spring to the kitchen for a meal, and then the unused part returned to the cooling water.

Even though the Brays were able to build a new home, farming had only a slight improvement. The threshing season was an exciting time for the community, especially for the youngsters. They loved seeing the big John Deere steel wheel tractor and the big metal threshing machine. Each farmer helped three farms before his threshing and three farms after. They would converge on the farm with wagons pulled by mules, horses, or a few farm tractors. The big John Deere tractor sat facing the harvester with a long, flat ten-inch-wide belt transmitting power to the harvester. Loaded wagons sat on either side and men threw grain sheaves onto the conveyor. Metal fingers pulled the sheaves into the big machine, so it could extract the grain to grain-bags and blow the straw onto a large stack.

One day Eric agreed to stack oat sheaves on a wagon with two neighbor men pitching up the bundles. If the worker on the wagon was watchful, he could succeed in stacking a large load. Eric piled the grain-head outward and the stalk inward, then he secured the load by a layer in the middle. As the stacker built the load, the outside circumference decreased. The men in Eric's community took pride in all farm work. They had a way of stacking baled hay or grain sheaves—not only to look good but to stabilize the load. Eric had placed the sheaves for about one-half load when he heard the two men below say, "Let's really work Eric hard."

The man on the ground usually throws one sheave at a time to give the person on the wagon time to accurately place them. After saying this, both thrust their five-prong pitchfork into the oat shock then heaved the entire collection of sheaves onto the wagon. The shocks were close together, so the men on the ground had ample supply to throw Eric more sheaves than he had time to stack. Eric worked fast but was unable to place them; after the third bunch, Eric asked them to slow down. Hearing another comment, Eric started pitching the sheaves off the other side of the wagon, making a long two-hundred-foot continuous row.

One man walked to the rear of the wagon and yelled, "Eric, what are you doing?"

Eric looked over the edge and said, "I told you I couldn't stack them, so I threw them off the other side."

The tractor driver, Coy, a church deacon, turned in his seat and gave Eric a thumbs up.

Women of the three farmers that Eric's dad helped thresh their grain before his and the ladies of the three farms after, assisted Eric's mother in providing a pitch-in dinner for the entire gathering. The tractors were shut off, the horse stock watered and fed, and hand-washing took place close to the well. A tub of water sat on a low table with several hand towels and wash pans nearby. Before dinner, the group, including children, gathered in the yard to give God thanks for the laborers, safety, and the food. During the meal, some adult would mention the verse of Galatians 6:9 (KJV): "let us not be weary in well doing, for in due season we will reap (a harvest)." Everyone knew that God blessed the families not only with a bountiful harvest of the land but also, they would reap spiritually. About the middle of the afternoon, the workers were served with watermelon, cantaloupe, cookies, and other homemade treats. At the end of the day, the expressions of satisfaction and happiness overwhelmed the group. There were a few tears, several hugs, and a lot of long-lasting handshakes. Everyone was tired, but they cheerfully returned home.

Corn shucking occurred when a family fell behind in the harvest due to sickness or some other unforeseen circumstance. Usually, the men distributed portions of the shock in small bunches on the ground in a circular pattern. Those present knelt beside one bundle and removed the ear corn, throwing it to a pile in the middle. When all the fodder was carried to the barn, and the piles of corn were thrown into a wagon pulled by mules, then the corn was unloaded in the crib. If enough help showed up at a shucking, several clusters made a picturesque scene, especially in newly fallen snow. A few hours of shucking corn made one hungry. Mealtime brought sharing delicious food, joy, and bonding of friendships that lasted many years.

A road repair detail brought loads of rock to fill soft places or redo a section of washed-out road. The stones were gathered from crop fields, along small streams or creeks. Men cleaned ditches and culverts with shovels to ensure proper drainage. The county government improved its road department, but it still lacked adequate resources, leaving each community on its own to repair the public roads. Frequently while Eric and Tom removed rocks in cultivated fields, they discussed 2 Kings 3:19 (KJV). After the Israelite's victory, they were to "mar every good piece of land with stones" by piling rocks on their enemies' fields. To them, this seemed an unusual victory phenomenon.

When a loved one died, after embalming, the body was returned home for an all-night vigil. Neighbors and friends who expressed condolences brought food, and a group would linger all night. The men of the community always dug graves. Gathering at the gravesite, each person, young or old, took turns to form the width and length of the grave. Placement and measurements had to be exact to ensure no disturbance of the adjoining burial space. The diggers placed the excavated soil carefully on a tarp for later use in closing the grave or filling it if it sank. The family buried the body in a well-constructed wooden casket with a layer of thick white oak hardwood boards placed directly over it.

As an average healthy teenager growing up in a rural community in southern Kentucky, Eric seldom formed a quick opinion about a new acquaintance or an unusual situation. Many in the neighborhood saw Eric as a placid, bashful, and modest boy. Their idea of him did not change when he became a teenager. His part in group discussions consisted of impartial listening with excellent retention. During Eric's early childhood, he experienced problems in the pronunciation of many formal or vernacular language sounds. No accolades came his way. He deliberately developed the unhurried formation of an opinion. Eric indignantly recalled many adult conversations. Raised eyebrows and slight smiles hid by a raised hand over or near the mouth never escaped its meaning. When disappointment or discouragement came his way as a child, preteen, or teenager, a digressive trip was necessary for him to realign his thinking from an emotional hurt to the obsequiously love of nature.

Oftentimes Eric laid in a soft bed of wild grass admiring the puffy white clouds as they floated by high in the blue sky. He often marveled at the picturesque heavens, imagining them as being ethereal, especially the small ones. Sometimes the lower azure clouds raced toward the east faster than the higher clouds. It seemed as if they were in a contest to see which was the fastest. Coming together, they occasionally reminded Eric of a familiar animal or tree shape. During certain weather conditions, gorgeous colors framed the clouds, beautifying them even more. He recalled the Scripture the preacher quoted from King David, Psalm 57:5 (KJV), something like, "let thy glory be above all the earth." Eric certainly described some of these scenes as "glorious."

CHAPTER 2

THE WATERFALL

ERIC BRAY LIVED WITH HIS FAMILY ON A rural farm north of the Pulaski County Seat of Somerset, Kentucky. Besides his parents, Elbert and Mabel, he also resided with his seventeen-year-old brother, Tom, and a fifteen-year-old sister, Julie. Tom is a high school senior and Julie, a freshman. With school beginning in late August, Eric, now thirteen and turning fourteen in February, would ride a bus with his brother and sister to Eubank to enroll in the seventh grade. At age four, a doctor diagnosed Eric as having Ankyloglossia, a mild form of tongue manipulation. Due to this problem of language enunciation, Eric repeated the first grade. It was difficult for him to convey the meaning of an assignment or convince his teacher that he understood math. When Eric answered questions, the teacher's expression was ambiguous with a frown and then a slight smile and asked Eric to repeat. At the youthful age of six, he could not understand why she could not accept his answers;

his answers were the same as the other children in his class.

Several people in the community, especially one family, snickered at the way he pronounced certain words describing interactions with other children. When it happened at large church gatherings, it was quite disconcerting. A neighbor imitated Eric's incorrect phonation; then his spouse mimicked it. They always ended their exhibition with a repugnant mindless smile. The older he grew, the angrier Eric became with each embarrassing, humiliating, hurtful, and numbing incident. Crestfallen because of these cruel insinuations and comments, Eric's obsession with nature became his panacea.

Completing the sixth grade at Estes Elementary School in northern Pulaski County, Eric continued his friendship and adventurous excursions with his close friend, Ron Milford. Eugene West, a relative of Eric's, became the third member of the triad. They busied themselves during the summer aiding their respective family in planting, tilling, and harvesting the many farm products. For Eric, these products were tobacco, sorghum, strawberries, milk, eggs, fryers, and veal calves. The Brays had a sizable amount of vegetables growing in their garden: beans, potatoes, tomatoes, sweet potatoes, onions, radishes, bib lettuce, cabbage, carrots, cucumbers, cantaloupes, watermelons, peanuts, sweet corn, popcorn, and eight-row white corn. The eight-row white corn was ground into cornmeal or made into hominy. Gardening and storing corn and hay for animal feed required extra work.

The summer work began in early March. Burning of large brush piled high on last year's tobacco plant bed destroyed any weed seed left behind. Logs, six-inches in diameter, positioned around the rectangular area, supported cotton canvas. The planting of tobacco, cabbage, radish, Early Boy tomato, and bib lettuce seed in the prepared bed soil took place by late March. The canvas gave a blanket of warmth protecting the tiny tender emerging seed during cold spring weather. Transplanting these plants in a tobacco patch or garden took place when the weather became warm. Planting of field corn and sorghum cane in fields plowed by mules in January took place by the tenth of April. It was customary, if weather allowed, to plant all garden and field crops by the fifteenth of May. While these crops grew, the family picked and sold strawberries from the one-acre plot. During the long summer, while Eric worked the garden or fields, he longed for a retreat at the beautiful waterfall in the secluded spot two miles south on Barney's Branch. Someday, he wanted to visit the dangerous and mysterious Culhwich cave beyond the waterfall.

After selling most of the strawberries, Eric took advantage of the decrease in crop cultivation and took solitude trips in the woods. One evening after supper, he walked the half-mile to his favorite woody dale, where he wandered from tree to tree. Viewing these magnificent trees always gave comfort to his soul. In the dwindling twilight, as he sat at the base of a huge white oak tree, he recalled the story of Abimelech in Judges 9:1-15 (KJV). Jotham, the youngest of seventy half-brothers, escaped Abimelech's murderous episode of sixty-nine of them; he then made a speech on Mount Gerizim. He used the comparison of making the olive tree, the fig tree, or the grapevine to be a king. He contrasted these three that gave useful commodities to the people, to a useless thorn bush. The only thing it provided was a pain; Abimelech, the thorn bush, was not pleased with the speech. As Eric sat there thinking about this story, and Jotham using the trees, as an illustration, he thought, *how could anyone use this beautiful tree to depict horrible human interactions?* This tree was much older than he, his father, or his papaw. A thought crossed his mind as he sat against the massive trunk: *I should write a poem sometime about "The Mighty Oak."*

With chores done, one late afternoon during the summer of 1954 before Eric entered the seventh grade, he loaded his backpack with its usual stuff: fishing hook and string, metal folding drinking cup, his trusted five-inch sharp blade Kentucky Hunting knife, a pair of old leather gloves, ten-foot small nylon rope, and a large metal tent peg. Hanging from the bottom of his backpack was his trusty all-steel hatchet and old army binoculars. Dangling from the torn denim hip pocket hung a homemade slingshot. As he passed through the kitchen, he picked up a baked Irish potato and a cold homemade biscuit.

"Mom, I'll eat when I get back."

"Where are you going this late?" she asked.

"It will be a full moon tonight, and I want to see the waterfall," Eric answered. "I'm going by the Milford's; Ron will probably want to go. It might be late when I get back, so don't worry."

"Are you taking Eugene with you?"

"Not tonight. I'll ask him some other time."

"Do you have a flashlight?"

"I won't need one; the moon will be bright enough to see. I want to see the honeysuckle vine bloom in the moonlight mist. It will be beautiful."

"You be careful," she counseled him.

"Okay."

Picking up his contorted walking stick, he jumped off the back porch and slipped past the trail-ready old box farm wagon. It sat in the bay of the two-story woodhouse building waiting for an axle repair from the Wainwright. Raising his stick over his head, he squeezed by the wagon. Walking down the lane and gravel road, he arrived at the Milford's; Ron met him in the yard.

"Do you want to go to the waterfall?" Eric asked.

"Now?"

"Yes," Eric replied.

"I sure do. I'll get my stick and a flashlight," Ron quickly answered.

"Get your walking stick; you won't need a flashlight."

"Why?"

"It is a cloudless night, and with a full moon we can see virtually as good as in daylight."

As the boys strolled through the hay field to the branch, Ron said, "Eric, will you help me find a stick like yours sometime?"

"You bet I will."

"How does it get its shape?" quizzed Ron.

"A wild poison oak vine or grapevine wraps itself around a sapling, and as it matures, the vine restricts the healthy growth of the tree. Each year, as the vine grows upward, it encircles the trunk attaching itself to the young bark, gripping it tight. In a few years, the small Elm tree has a twisted appearance and is ready for the removing of the vine and bark. The close adherence of the vine gives the little tree an abnormal form, concave spiral grooves from top to bottom," explained Eric.

"Where can we look for a sapling like that?" quizzed Ron.

"We'll look around the creek bank or on the peripheries of timber."

Reaching the concrete culvert, they slipped over the grassy bank into the creek bed. As they walked along the creek in the bright moonlight, Eric inspected the new growth of Mayapples, hazelnut bushes, hickory nut, and black walnut trees. When he examined the egg-shaped pale green fruit hanging from a knee-high plant, Ron asked, "What is that?"

"It's called a Mayapple, or some people call them American Mandrakes," Eric answered. "You can eat the ripe flesh, but my papaw says the seeds are poisonous. The fruit has a lot of large seeds; I don't like to eat them. If you want, we'll come back in late fall to gather nuts for winter storage. Some winters we've harvested two bushels of hickory nuts and black walnuts."

"I've eaten store-bought black walnuts, but I don't think I've ever eaten hickory nuts," Ron said.

Eric asked, "Did you ever pick up a dark walnut hull and it leaves your hand stained?"

"Yes, I did once, and I couldn't wash it off. It had to wear off."

"You know the walnut hulls are used to make different shades of dye, from tan to deep brown."

"Really? Mother loves walnut furniture, and she has several picture frames made of walnut," Ron answered.

"Mother is especially fond of the thin-shell 'pecan hickory nuts,'" informed Eric. "The kernels are similar in size, shape, and taste to pecans. She even makes fake pecan pies using the thin-shell nuts."

Moving on down the creek, they passed the community swimming hole. The very first trip with his new friend Ron, they came upon some older neighbor kids swimming naked. He recalled how embarrassed they were when they peeked through the hazelnut bushes.

Continuing downstream to the waterfall, they sat on the edge of the plateau with feet hanging over the edge, just above the water. Putting their hands on the ground behind them, they leaned back to gaze skyward through the soft twilight at a full mid-summer moon. Neither spoke.

The scene was idyllic. Eric sat there, with his eyes closed, private in thought, waves of joy rippled through his whole body. "Thank you, God, for such beauty and serenity," he prayed. "Thank you for creating it and permitting me to enjoy it." He sat there a long time enjoying the incredible fragranced soft breeze flowing across the spectacular misty waterfall. The mist generated at the base, rose slowly upward, dispersing into the air by movement of the water flowing over the thirty-foot waterfall. The fog drifted across a few late honeysuckle flowers, then disappeared. Eric breathed the clean, fresh air into his lungs which gave his soul a blessing, peace, and contentment.

A noise suddenly came from his right. "Did you just pray?"

Opening his eyes, Eric had utterly forgotten Ron. A little embarrassed, he began to apologize. "I'm sorry Ron. I was caught up in the enjoyment, the smell, and the tranquility of the waterfall," Eric answered.

"The beauty of the waterfall at night has to be more picturesque than in daylight," Ron remarked. "Why is it so bright? I have never been out at night with a full moon. This is neat." Caught up in the serenity of the mist floating through rays of the full moon, he had already forgotten his first question.

"Well, the moon's closeness to the earth makes it look larger and brighter, as it reflects the sun's light," Eric answered. "Look at the shimmering glow on the far west scattered stratus clouds. It allows stars to shine through the silvery vapors next to the clouds, producing an indescribable depiction of nature, don't you think?"

"Breathless," whispered Ron.

Seeing the wholesome and unrestricted enjoyment, Eric was thankful he had brought him. *Someday*, he thought, *I will talk to him about becoming a Christian*. Even though Ron showed interest in the Bible and his family had attended church regularly, he did not want to overwhelm him too soon.

However, Eric, with some hesitation, wanted to plant a small seed, so he said, "Let's thank God together."

To his surprise, Ron answered, "Okay, how?"

"Since we have seen the intense beauty, let us bow our heads for a few seconds and then we will raise our hands toward Heaven, thanking God for this blessing," suggested Eric. "Will that be okay with you?"

"Sure, let's do it," Ron quickly answered.

They bowed their heads for a few seconds, raised their hands toward Heaven, and to Eric's surprise, he heard two heartfelt "thanks." He did not expect Ron to take part.

Getting to his feet, Eric said, "We had better start back."

"What time is it?" Ron asked.

"I reckon it is about eleven o'clock."

"I didn't think you had a wristwatch," Ron said.

"I don't but look at those rain clouds in the far west. It will take the moon another five or six hours to go down beyond the horizon, so it is an hour or so before midnight."

Retrieving their backpacks and walking sticks, the boys started upstream. Moving around a fallen white oak log, a mother opossum toting five babies clinched to her back, wandered out of the labyrinth trails under the wild blackberry thicket. As she approached the boys, she stopped and turned to hiss, baring white shiny teeth. The little one clinging in front of its siblings languished a similar snarl but showed no teeth.

"Let's sit on the log and watch them for a little while," Eric suggested.

They sat down on the fallen log to watch the little mother and her family.

"The little ones are so cute with their hairless tail, staring dark eyes, and a shiny pink nose," Ron pointed out. "Look, they are about the size of a well-fed mouse."

"Ron, she will carry them on her back for about two months. I am sure that little mother knows where that tall persimmon tree stands between Dad's garage and barn. Persimmons are a favorite autumn fare for the opossum," informed Eric.

Starring at these large humans who showed no imminent threat, she turned and ambled around the rotting pile of limbs and disappeared into the underbrush.

The duo avoids the opossum family and moved upstream about five hundred feet when a faint grunting sound came from the adjacent woods.

"Did you hear that?" quizzed Ron.

Putting his finger to his lips, Eric indicated that both should stop and be silent. The sound echoed through the fresh night air; then a loud scratching noise. Ron looked at Eric, shrugged his shoulders, and smiled.

In a few minutes, a raccoon nursery came out of the hazelnut thicket and marched by in single file. The mother raccoon simply glanced at Eric and Ron, then led her three youngsters across the path and continued over the bank to the shallow stream.

"Aren't raccoons normally nocturnal animals that will eat about anything? Have you ever had a raccoon as a pet?" Ron inquired.

"Yes, they are nocturnal and no I've never had a pet raccoon."

"Do they always wash their food?" Ron continued.

"A lot of people say that the raccoon washes its food, but Papaw says they rub their food to remove debris or dirt. Often people see them around water, so they think the raccoons wash all their food," Eric said.

Not thinking any more of the family, they proceeded upstream, and in a few minutes reached the concrete culvert. Climbing the bank to the gravel road, they made their way home lit by a full mid-summer moon.

Arriving at his driveway, Ron said, "Eric, I enjoyed tonight, thanks."

Eric knew the response came straight from the heart. "I enjoyed it too; we'll do it again soon."

Leaving his trusty walking stick on the porch, Eric entered the kitchen. As he removed his backpack, the baked potato and biscuit fell to the floor.

"I thought you were going to eat those; did you forget you had food?"

"Yes, I guess I did," answered Eric. "You should have seen the mist in the moonlight at the waterfall; it is hard to describe the peace and contentment that came over me while I was sitting there under a full moon. Mom, you have to see it sometime."

"Boy, there is no lack of enthusiasm," she said. "Your supper is on the table. I heard your jingling coming up the road, so I heated your supper; do you want milk to drink?"

"No Mom, I'll just drink water."

"Eat your supper and go to bed. It is getting late, and you have a big work day tomorrow."

CHAPTER 3

THE BLUE RACER

THE NEXT MORNING ERIC FINISHED HIS morning chores. He and Tom, his older brother by four years, were assigned to chop the weeds from the cornfield. Gathering hoes from the shed, they walked the gravel road for a mile to the ten-acre field just above a northwestern tributary of Barney Branch. The water entered the larger stream just north of the massive concrete culvert. During heavy rains, converging of the two waterways flooded the adjacent low farmland.

Starting at the top of the field, they walked the baulks removing weeds. Making several trips across the corn patch, they paused to take a break in a large mowed area at the field's entrance. Refreshing themselves with a drink from a water jug, they sat down to rest.

"You know Tom, there are only a few weeds in this corn, and it probably doesn't need chopping."

Tom declared, "You know Dad, he requires us to remain busy; remember his mantra, 'An idle mind is the devil's workshop.'"

"Dad should have been a Chief Executive Officer of a huge company; he believes everyone should work, work, work," laughed Eric.

"You're correct about that."

The next few minutes they recounted the numerous jobs that consumed countless hours during the summer; they even recalled scores of hours of arduous work last summer and the summer before that.

"Tom, remember two years ago when we helped Dad and Uncle Henry move the voting house? That was a lot of hard hot work, wasn't it?"

Tom said, "It was dangerous, too."

The county government permitted Eric's dad to move the voting house from the wooded area to an unused spot in the church's parking lot. Many years ago, Eric's grandfather authorized part of the woods as the community voting place. It had adequate space for parking buggies and tying horses to trees, but with modern road improvement, its new location was more accessible to those who had automobiles. Raising the little single-room building to place round logs under the six-by-six runners, proved to be an enormous job. It had to be rolled on six logs placed under the wood foundation, moved straight out of the trees onto a gravel road, turned, and then pulled down the hill. Thick chimney sandstones placed near holes dug beneath the runners, supported pry logs to raise the structure. With the six logs evenly spaced under the building, a heavy-duty chain hooked to the little MT John Deere tractor; the building began the long, arduous journey to its new site. As it moved forward, the building came off the log at the rear; the exposed log had to be quickly moved to the front, for continuous rolling support. After moving it to the road, it had to be turned, and when it neared the hill descent, another log had to be placed against the building and the tractor. This log between the building and tractor prevented it from rolling forward off the logs and losing control while traveling downhill. Prying up the building to replace the logs under it in the narrow gravel road, would have been difficult.

Taking another drink from the water jug, Eric said, "Boy, I don't even want to think about moving that building again, it took all day."

Rising, they retrieved their hoes and proceeded to the next row.

"Tom, look! A black snake!"

"Where?"

"It just came off the bank. Boy, it looks almost blue," Eric yelled, pointing at the snake.

"Maybe, it is what Dad calls a 'racer.'"

As they stood talking about it, the snake slithered toward them a few feet and elevated its head eight inches above the ground. Being unafraid of snakes, Eric, hoe in hand, shuffled a few steps closer. There was no movement of the snake; Eric took one more step.

"Eric, leave that snake alone, it's not harming any-thing. If it is a 'racer,' you just might see it race firsthand."

Ignoring Tom's warning, Eric took another step toward the snake. Suddenly, the snake slid a few feet toward him, stopped, and raised its head even higher. This time the head was twelve-inches high, and it moved slowly back and forth.

"Eric, you're asking for it. I hope it chases you all the way across the field," commented Tom.

"Oh, don't worry Tom, I was just toying with it," answered Eric.

Tom said, "Come on, let's get back to work. We need to complete this entire field by dinner."

Glancing at the snake one more time, Eric shrugged his shoulders and turned to focus on the next baulk. The first step away from the snake triggered it to slither toward him.

Tom yelled, "Run Eric, that snake is after you."

Caught off guard, Eric jumped. Looking over his shoulder, he released the hoe handle, dropping it to the ground. Impulsively he ran; Tom laughed, and seeing the snake close behind, yelled again, "Run, Eric run." As Eric increased his first move into a full run, the "racer" stayed right behind. Tom was ecstatic now, whooping and yelling, "Run, Eric, run!" Thoughtless, Eric sprinted into the open mowed area. Remembering the hoe laying on the ground some distance away, and the snake close behind, he began circling the sizable area back toward his gleeful brother. Tom now stood motionless, with his hoe raised, ready for a strike. Eric, a thirteen-year-old teenager, at a full run, outdistanced the snake by five yards. As he approached Tom, he yelled, "Get him, Tom, get him!" As he passed, one swift strike by Tom and the chase was over. Unfortunate for the pursuer, fortunate for the pursued.

Sliding to a stop, Eric said, "Boy, what about that! I thought stories about 'racers' were just legends."

"Like the hoop snake."

"Yeah," Eric answered.

"I thought you weren't afraid of snakes."

"I'm not, but I didn't know what to do, and I dropped my hoe," he answered.

"Boy, I can't wait to tell our cousins about this," announced Tom.

"Yeah, I bet they will take pleasure in hearing about it, and you will have great enjoyment telling them."

"Why didn't you stop and grab it by the head like you did the one in the chicken house?"

"I didn't have time. You yelled run, so I ran," answered Eric.

The snake episode was over, so they finished hoeing the corn and walked the gravel road home. During the chores that evening, Tom reminded Eric of the snake chasing him. As Tom milked a cow in a stall next to Eric, Tom retold his version of the chase. "Dad, you should have seen Eric run; he was running and jumping at the same time; it was hilarious to watch."

"Eric, I thought you were not afraid of snakes."

Eric answered, "I'm not, Dad, but Tom yelled 'run' so I ran."

A few minutes later, Tom mentioned the blue racer again. At the end of the comment, he reached under his cow with a tobacco stick and gently touched Eric's backside. Eric's sudden movement triggered "Old Betsy" to kick; the half-full bucket landed upside down on Eric's knees spilling the contents onto his blue jeans and into his high-top work-boots.

"You boys behave," came from the stable across the barn gangway. Dad was assisting a newborn calf with its first meal; the Jersey heifer refused to claim her first calf.

Tom laughed so hard the cow he was milking became nervous and kicked; he jerked the bucket free of her foot just in time.

The entire incident in the cornfield and the barn consumed the chitchat around the dinner table. Julie was ecstatic hearing about the chase and teasing. "Tom, what can I do to help?" she asked him as they moved away from the table; Eric had already left the house to close the chicken house door.

"I want to put a pokeweed stalk in his bed tonight; it is cool, slick, and about the same size as a snake; Want to help?"

"Tell me how," she answered.

Tom said, "He'll be watching me, so can you go get a stalk about three feet long?"

"Where do I find it?"

"There's a plant behind the corncrib. Get it, take it upstairs, and put it under the sheet at the foot of the bed."

Later in the evening, as Eric moved up the steps, Tom touched his leg and said, "Snake, snake." Each time, Eric kicked backward. Tom wanted to keep the snake chase fresh in his memory.

Reaching the top, Eric turned and said, "What is your problem?"

"Oh, I don't know, I just enjoyed watching you run from that snake so much, I won't ever forget it," Tom answered smiling.

As they prepared for bed, Tom had one more prompt, "Eric, I caught that blue racer and put it in your bed."

"Sure, you did. I'm soooo afraid of snakes," Eric said sarcastically.

Julie had sneaked to the top step, just outside of the door, ready to take part in the jollity when Eric covered himself with the sheet.

Eric swung his feet up into the bed and pulled the sheet over his legs. His feet slid under the pokeweed stalk; its touching the ankle felt like a movement; he immediately moved, jumped, rolled, and fell onto the floor. Julie flipped the light on and while Eric laid on the floor, he watched her laugh harder than he had ever seen her laugh.

"That was the most hilarious movement I've ever seen," Tom said between bursts of laughter.

Julie continued giggling as she made her way down the steps.

Eric removed the long, smooth, slick purple stalk from his bed; it was past midnight before he fell asleep.

CHAPTER 4

BANANA-DONUT TREAT

WHILE EATING SUPPER ONE SATURDAY IN late August, Eric's mom said, "Did you kids know school will start in ten days?"

Julie spoke first, "Oh, I can't wait!"

Surprised, Mom said, "I didn't think you liked school."

"Oh, it's okay, I guess. If I must, I'll go."

Clearing his throat, Dad glanced across the table and announced, "Young lady, it is a must."

When Dad spoke, Julie dared not roll her eyes or answer with a verbal response. One of Dad's mantras was, "All of you will graduate from high school; if I have to, I'll take you to class myself."

"Julie could your sudden interest in school be your attraction to Larry, Ron's brother?" questioned Tom.

Julie came back with, "I suppose you like school because of that blond-head from upstate New York, huh?"

Eric sat quietly eating a bowl of Mother's home-made vegetable-beef soup. Crumbles of partially submerged cornbread floated on top. Next to his favorite soup sat a large glass of fresh buttermilk. During the conversation, he stayed silent. When everyone finished, and the table cleared, Eric went outside. Scratching his head as he stepped off the porch, he mumbled to himself, "I can't believe they didn't ask me about school, if I wanted to go, or if I was excited about riding the bus, or even if I was glad to be going with Ron."

Forgetting about school, he wandered across the yard to the purple martin's pole, positioned near the garden fence. A steel pole supported the white aluminum birdhouse twelve feet above the ground. Usually, twelve pairs nested in mid-April and raise two or three chicks. During feeding, the little six to seven-inch-long insectivores became boisterous, especially at twilight. They fluttered, squawked, and in Eric's opinion, even protested going to roost.

Eric enjoyed watching the little "flying insect grab-bers" gather for the nightly roost. Sometimes they dive-bombed him, not wanting to attack but to say hello. These little birds nested close to human residences. When Eric walked through grassland disturbing hopping or flying insects, the purple martins swooped around him picking off the unfortunate. When several tried to capture a snack at the same moment, often one would brush his clothing.

Tonight, it was much quieter than usual. It was late August, and most of the little ones had grown strong enabling them to fly the long journey south. One pair either hatched late or had a weak one unable to fly. The devoted couple would not leave until it was able to fly, or it succumbed to sickness.

Taking one last look, he turned and went back to the house.

During the Friday evening meal, Mom said, "Elbert, don't you think we should go to Somerset tomorrow? We need to buy school supplies for the kids."

Turning to Tom and Eric, she asked, "What do you need?"

"Mom, I need a few things too," Julie quickly inserted into the conversation.

"Julie, I know you need some things, you and I will go to Woolworth's department store or the 5 & 10 store," Mom replied.

"Mom, I don't need anything, except maybe a pair of socks. You know I got two pairs of pants and three shirts from my Indiana cousins."

"I just need to look," Tom was quick to reply.

Saturday morning the family loaded into the 1949 flatbed farm truck for the eighteen-mile trip to the county seat. Dad, Mom, and Julie rode inside, Tom and Eric had to ride on a bale of straw right behind the cab. Wooden cattle racks on the flatbed gave some protection from the whirling wind, but Tom still worried that his hair would become messed up. Eric didn't worry about his flattop haircut.

Arriving in town, Dad pulled into the A&P Food Store parking lot. As he got out of the parked truck, he said, "I'm going to the bank, then the courthouse." Everyone knew Dad liked to talk about politics, and the courthouse was an excellent place to engage in a federal, state, or local discussion.

"Julie, you and I will go to Woolworth first, then to the 5 & 10. Boys, you know where to go, so we'll see you back here in about one hour, okay?" Mom informed them.

Tom bought two pants, a pocket comb, and a small bottle of Vaseline hair tonic to give his hair a slick-wet look. Eric bought two pairs of black socks at the 5 & 10. After purchasing the items, they decided to return to the truck. As they passed a bakery, a customer opened the door letting out a tantalizing warm aroma that floated across the sidewalk. Both stopped, looked at each other, and at once, dived for the door. They hurried in and bought a dozen warm glazed doughnuts that was cooked early that morning for twenty-five cents. Rushing back to the A&P food store, Tom took the doughnuts to the truck, and Eric entered the store to buy bananas. Surveying the fruit counter, he chose six overripe bananas. Taking them to the checkout for weighing, the store clerk said, "Son, that will be ten cents."

"Thanks," Eric said as he paid the cashier.

Arriving at the truck, he and Tom moved across the gravel parking lot to a shaded area. Sitting cross-legged on a narrow grassy area by the fence, they each consumed three bananas and six donuts. A bite of banana, a bite of donut.

"Hum, this is good," Tom uttered.

Eric said with a mouthful, "You better believe it."

As Eric and Tom grew older, they could not under-stand why this was such a treat. Was it the sweetness, the fruit, the personal purchase, or the combination of taste? The Bray's household always had jams, jellies, honey, and molasses setting on the dining table. All kinds of sweet canned fruit like cold-packed apples, pickled peaches, and semi-sweetened blackberries sat beside the array of homegrown and canned foodstuff. It was seldom that Mom did not serve some sort of pie, cake, cookies, or bread pudding for dessert at the end of the meal. On rare occasions, Mom served "pig in the blanket," a specialty of sweetened and seasoned dried apples wrapped in a thin baked pie shell and served with a thicken cinnamon milk poured over the top. There was no shortage of sweets in the Bray family.

Dad concluded banking and politicking. Mom and Julie finished shopping. Tom and Eric, full, started the eighteen-mile trip home.

Exiting the truck, Mom said, "Okay, it's time for dinner, give me about thirty minutes, and it will be ready."

Eric glanced at Tom and said, "Mom, I don't think we'll eat."

"Why not?"

"Oh, we're just not hungry," Tom answered.

"Okay boys grab your hoes and work the garden; it will take you most of the afternoon," Dad instructed.

Eric and Tom discovered overripe bananas and glazed donuts did little for stamina. They experienced a lack of energy by two o'clock. Tom spoke as his stomach growled, "Boy, I wish I'd eaten dinner."

"Me too," uttered Eric.

CHAPTER 5

SEVENTH GRADE, A NEW EXPERIENCE

(1954-55) SCHOOL STARTED TUESDAY morning after Labor Day. Going to school with friends was a reprieve from hard farm work. The old international bus traveled the twisting gravel roads throughout the community picking up mostly eager children, but a few were unenthusiastic. The front and back steel wheels supported retreaded tires—three of the six had dry-rot cracks. A part of the retreaded rubber was missing on top of the right front tire. When the driver changed gears, a puff of black smoke exhausted through the tailpipe. The children, nor anyone in the community, thought much about it; the bus was still running, and the tires were not flat. The oldest model in the county's fleet required the driver to open the door and manually engage the stop sign. The traffic stop sign had to be levered open by the driver. If he forgot, it didn't matter; few motorized vehicles traveled the narrow roads.

The driver, Junior Brooks, struggled in shifting gears with his injured arm and hand. Eric liked watching him double-clutch, slightly race the gasoline engine, and ram the transmission into a faster or lower speed.

Junior loved driving the bus and interacting with the children, especially the young ones. Many times, throughout the year, he offered everyone candy, especially before Christmas. The Brays, Tom, Julie, and this year, Eric, were to decline the candy politely. Everyone knew that Junior was not financially well-off, so they settled only for his endearments. He greeted everyone with a smile and welcomed them to "come aboard."

Eric, Tom, and Julie stood by the road waiting for the bus. It was 6:30 in the morning and a slight fog clung close to the ground resisting disbursement by the predicted sun that was partially visible over the woods. Tom's hair was slick with Vaseline hair tonic and a black comb stuck out of his shirt pocket. Julie wore a new cotton floral dress, new shoes, and a unique hairstyle. Eric stood there nervous in his high-top work shoes and wore a cousin's well-worn hand-me-down trousers. Climbing aboard, Tom, a senior, sat in the middle, while Julie headed for the rear seat. Eric plopped down on the front seat. He wanted to save a place for Ron; his house was the next stop. Traveling down the road, crossing the branch, shifting into a lower gear for the hill, Junior stopped in front of Milford's house. The doors swung open. "Come aboard," Junior bade with the predictable toothy smile.

"I saved you and Eugene a seat," Eric informed Ron. As Ron sat beside him, Eric noticed Tom inviting Larry to sit with him. He was glad to see his brother befriend their new neighbor; he had shown little prior interest in making Larry's acquaintance.

The next stop was the West's.

"Thanks," Ron said as he sat down. "Do you know our new teachers?"

"No, but I've heard that one of our seventh-grade teachers is Mrs. Wilson. Everyone says she is an outstanding teacher."

The yellow student transport stopped at the West's, and Junior said, "Come aboard, Eugene."

The trio shared summer activities as they continued to a new school, to different friends.

Between the Good Hope community and Eubank, the bus crossed Buck Creek on an old, dilapidated, rusty steel bridge. Some of the bridge's white-oak two-by-six flooring boards were loose, several twisted, and others warped. A rusty white sign stood boldly in front of the entrance warning travelers: "Two-ton limit."

As the bus approached the bridge, Ron asked, "Why are we stopping?"

"Tom tells me that the bus loaded with children is too heavy to cross, so we will have to get off and walk across."

With eyebrows drawn down, Ron said, "You are kidding me, right?"

"Okay, everyone off," yelled Junior, "You know the drill."

As the threesome moved toward the open door, Eric came back with, "Ron, does that answer your question?"

As they walked across the bridge, Ron said, "I suppose we get back on when the bus pulls across, right?"

"That's right."

"What will we do if the bridge buckles under the weight of the empty bus and it falls into the creek?"

"I guess we will either walk to school or go back home," answered Eric.

"How do we get back across the creek? It's deep," Ron said.

Eric responded with, "Boy, you are full of questions this morning, aren't you?"

Eugene just stood there smiling, listening to the questions and answers.

The bus inched slowly across the squeaky bridge, the steel beams moaning, the wooden flooring popping, both protesting their load. During the noisy crossing, Ron turned and said, "Boy, I'm glad we didn't ride that bus across. Those steel beams are rusty, and one has a hole in it. Hey, what happens when it rains?"

"I guess we will get wet," Eric said, grinning.

When the bus successfully crossed, all twenty-seven students retook their seats; then the bus had to climb a narrow, rough hill laden with large limestone outcroppings. As it climbed the rocky hill, the children were in trepidation of the bus slipping sideways and plunging into the gorge. It arrived in Eubank at 8:20 with forty-two children.

"You seventh graders go to that building," Junior said as he pointed to a double-room building behind the two-story brick high school. The building had been built shortly after World War II with post-war materials.

"Thanks, Mr. Brooks," Ron said before Eric or Eugene could speak.

Mounting the steps, they hesitantly stepped into a small classroom. An older girl, Eric assumed her to be a senior student, approached them and said, "Take a seat on that front row; your teacher, Mrs. Smith, will talk to you in a minute."

Taking their seat, Ron looked at Eric and mouthed the words, "I thought her name was Mrs. Wilson."

In a couple of minutes, the lady called Mrs. Smith, motioned with her hand, and said, "Come over here, boys. What are your names?"

"I'm Eric Bray, and these are my close friends and neighbors, Ron Milford and Eugene West."

"Hum, B, M, and W, Eric you will stay with me; Ron and Eugene will be in the other room with Mrs. Wilson," she informed them.

"We were hoping that we could stay together," Eric said.

"This is just for homeroom. We will group students according to the recommendation of your teacher last year," she replied. "Just have a seat, we'll start in a few minutes."

They chose seats near the front. Glancing at Eric, Ron noticed his countenance had changed. The squinted eyes, frowned wrinkles on his forehead, his taut mouth, and his set jaw revealed an apprehensive mien.

I wonder what she means by "grouping," Eric thought. *Is she going to ask if I repeated the first grade? Did I say something the wrong way? What did Mr. Walker, my sixth-grade teacher, tell her? Will she group me with others that have difficulty in enunciating words? Will I ever get rid of these bad feelings flashed across my mind?*

"Eric."

So, engrossed in the possibility of more hurtful comments and insinuations, he heard nothing.

"Eric," Ron repeated.

Turning, Eric said, "What, are you talking to me?"

"Is something wrong?"

"What do you mean?"

"Eric, you were in another world, is something wrong?" Ron asked.

"No, not really, I was just thinking about this new school."

He had never told Ron or Eugene about those ugly remarks made by adults that had hurt him so badly. Those words had prompted him to take long excursions in the thick woods or along the palisades of Barney's Branch. He concealed his feelings, not revealing them even to his parents. However, he sought the understanding and guidance of his grandfather. Eric's parents encouraged him to talk with older people because they understood what Job 12:12-13 (KJV) said about old people: "With the ancient (*traditions of the fathers*) is wisdom; and in length of days understanding. With Him (God) is wisdom and strength, He hath counsel and understanding." The wisdom and understanding the elderly learned from God were then transferred to Eric by example or by their teachings.

As the morning progressed, the students were welcomed. Mrs. Smith's homeroom had students with last names beginning with the letter A through L and Mrs. Wilson's homeroom, M through Z. Then the students were shown the location of well-water behind the high school building; the water was dispensed through a standard spigot. The restrooms were attached to the high school building, and the lunchroom building was located six hundred feet across campus. It sat on Eubank's main street, conspicuously alone of other school buildings. A rumor suggested the building had been a canning factory during World War II.

One day Eric asked permission to use the restroom. He opened the door and moved to the outside steps where he saw a gruesome sight. As Eric stood on the top level, a senior rushed by, groaning, supporting his mangled right hand with his left. His hand was bloody, and bones in his fingers were poking through the skin; he had a panicked expression on his pallid face as he ran to get help. The principal at once rushed him to the local doctor to seek medical aid. The injury occurred while using a powerful table saw in the agriculture shop beside the gym. The incident etched a memory that Eric would often recall.

The seventh grade quickly progressed to the three-week Christmas break. During the fall semester, Eric, Ron, and Eugene became close buddies on the bus, eating lunch, doing homework, and planning future excursions in the nearby countryside. The three loved the enticement of the palisades of Barney Branch. There was so much to see and explore along this small waterway in northern Pulaski County, including woods, thickets, abundant animal population, feet or body indentations for identifying the creatures, the swimming hole, the waterfall, and excellent camping spots. They also heard about many scuttlebutt activities of a man called "Weird Culhwich" in dark caves two miles south from the waterfall. He was a reticent individual who lived alone in his late parent's home and seldom engaged in an open conversation with neighbors. Whispered rumors quietly spoken, when near his relatives, told of the late Mr. Culhwich's disappearance for days in the small dangerous caves along the stream. The discussion about this rumor, while riding the bus to and from school, developed into an overnight camping plan for Eric, Ron, and Eugene. Even though the caves were unexplored and declared by older folks to be small and dangerous, the trio craved to see them.

CHAPTER 6

CHRISTMAS BREAK

ON THE WAY HOME FRIDAY AFTERNOON before starting Christmas break, the triad finalized plans for a camping trip on Monday night to the alleged caves. Arrangements with their brothers to do the evening chores allowed them to leave just after lunch.

On Monday, double-checking their backpacks, gathering more food, grabbing sleeping bags, picking up tightly rolled fabric, and their walking sticks, they excitedly began the well-planned journey. Slipping over the grassy road bank by the concrete culvert, Ron turned to Eric and said, "You know it was bizarre that our Sunday school lesson yesterday was about caves, wasn't it?"

"Yeah, I guess. I hadn't given it much thought," Eric responded.

Eugene asked, "Do you remember who it was about?"

"It was about Elijah and some other priest."

"Do you know which book and chapter that story is in?" quizzed Ron.

In mid-stride, Eric stopped, turned smiling and said, "Boy, you have a lot of questions today. You'll find that incident in Kings."

"It's in First Kings 18:4. They hid one hundred prophets in two caves, supplying them with bread and water," Ron answered.

"Do you remember why they were hidden?" questioned Eric.

"I sure do. That evil Jezebel, King Ahab's wife, was killing the Lord's prophets."

Eugene said, "You must have been paying close attention to remember all the details."

"I was, but I also went home and read the whole story, chapters sixteen through twenty-one," Ron humbly reported.

"That's good Ron. You know we should have brought a Bible with us."

Eugene responded with, "We'll have one on the next camping trip."

Wandering down the creek, from gravel bar to gravel bar, they picked up a few lingering nuts under the large black walnut tree, left by squirrels who did not need them as winter food. The well-used many trodden trails around the hazelnut thicket declared an active small animal population: raccoons, skunks, opossums, rabbits, and visiting beavers or muskrats. Passing the swimming hole, Eric said, "If beavers built a dam below this deep hole, it would double the depth, about five feet deep."

Ron asked, "Would it be safe to swim?"

"I'm sure it would, but Mom wouldn't like it."

Eugene added, "My mom wouldn't like it either."

They paused for a few minutes at the waterfall, then moved downstream to find a suitable camping site near the first cave. About one-and-three-quarters of a mile past the waterfall, they found a level open spot in a small pine clearing. A dead tree fifty feet south would provide firewood, fresh water gushed out of the limestone cliff just across the creek, and there were plenty of large stones at the water's edge to construct a safe cooking fire. Laying backpacks off, with walking sticks in hand, they moseyed to the first cave. Since it was late in the day, after examining the large entrance for thirty minutes, they decided to go back, set up camp, and explore the cave the next morning. Retracing their steps back to the campsite, they emptied their backpacks on a ten-foot square tarp. They set aside a larger twelve-foot square to use as a covering. Ron took two twenty-foot quarter-inch nylon ropes, and with Eric's help, they stretched both from pine tree to pine tree, eight-feet apart. The taut lines five feet above the ground supported the rain-proof fabric. Eric slip-knotted the two back corners and tied them low, forming a wall on the back of the shelter.

Eugene asked, "Why are you tying them so low?"

"The thick pine trees on each side and the fabric in the back tied to the ground will help prevent cool breezes from freezing us tonight." Pointing to a spot just in front of the fabric on the ground, he said, "We'll put the fire ring there, and we'll keep logs on the fire all night."

"Do you think it will get that cold?" Ron questioned.

"No, it is supposed to be seasonally warm, but you know, it's the middle of December, so it might get cold in the morning," Eric answered.

Eugene said, "I'll help Ron fix the fire ring." They gathered large round rocks and placed them close together in a three-foot circular pattern. Ron then took Eric's hatchet, cut two forked limbs from a bush, and drove the stakes into the ground just outside the ring of stones.

"Okay," Eric said as he picked up the hatchet, "I'm going to cut pine branches from those trees over there and place them between the trees and our sleeping bags, it will make our shelter warmer and cozier."

Gathering leaves and small dry twigs from the fallen tree a few feet away, Ron started a tepee fire. Returning to the log, he gathered larger limbs and piled them near the firestones. He then hung a small stainless-steel bucket from a horizontal pole supported by the vertical forked sticks on each side of the fire ring. He began cooking hotdogs in the container while Eric finished piling pine boughs around the campsite. Three large Idaho potatoes wrapped in aluminum foil baked just inside the fire-ring stones.

Sleeping bags laid open on the fabric floor. Personal items of the backpacks, such as folding drinking cups, metal pie plates, forks, spoons, toothbrushes and toothpaste, combs, and hunting knives had been lain neatly near the top of each sleeping bag.

Finishing his comfy efforts, Eric walked over to the fire, looked around, and said, "Boy Ron, you sure have been busy. What's for supper?"

"We've got us a real chef," Eugene said grinning.

"I've got hot dogs cooking in the pot, potatoes baking by the fire, and ready-to-eat fried apple pies your mom sent," Ron answered.

"Those are huge potatoes; where did you get them?"

"We grew them in our garden. It was the first garden I've ever worked in," Ron revealed.

"Well, good for you. Did you enjoy it?" quizzed Eric as he sat down near the fire.

"I did. Dad said that the chicken manure you helped Larry and me spread produced two bushels of these big potatoes."

Sitting cross-legged in front of the fire, with plates on their laps, they wolfed down the hotdogs wrapped with a barley and oat flatbread, baked spuds, fried dried apple pies, along with chilly sparkling water from the cliff. They cleaned all the utensils in a deep pool and laid them upside down on a pile of pine boughs.

Looking at Eric and Eugene positioning the silverware on the fresh pine, Ron asked, "Why are you laying them on the limbs?"

Eric answered, "Uncle Esau once told me the scent of a fresh cut pine limb would keep bugs away, we don't want bugs on our dishes."

Eugene suggested, "Let's eat some of those black walnuts we found."

"Good idea; here's the hatchet," Eric said as he handed it to him.

Cracking six walnuts revealed no kernels. Ron said, "I guess that tells us why the squirrels didn't need them for winter food; they know when a nut is empty."

Reclining on the sleeping bags, they lay there looking at the beautiful sunset on the western horizon. A faint crackling sound of burning wood drifted amongst the pine thicket, the smoke whorled in a spiral, then slowly rose in a twisted and con-voluted shape before disappearing. The smell of smoke mixed with the redolence of strongly scented pine resin released from the new cut branches. As they lay there enjoying the colossal and blissful heavenly panorama, no one spoke.

Laying with his hands behind his head, Eric finally asked, "Do either of you know how to locate the North Star?"

"I think you use the Big Dipper, some way," answered Ron. Pointing to the stars, he continued, "You can see most of them; the limbs conceal one star in the upper part of the bowl."

"Is a star in the Big Dipper, the North Star?"

Resuming his explanation, he said, "No, I don't think so, but you use the Dipper's bowl to locate it."

Eugene said, "I expect we'll learn about it when we start earth science after the Christmas break."

Feeling the warmth on their feet, relaxed and full, they were amazed by the celestial beauty. Eric wanted to talk to Ron about becoming a Christian but did not know how to start. He laid thinking that it would be best to speak to him when they were alone, but suddenly he asked, "Do you remember a star story in the Bible?"

"Didn't Joseph have a star in one of his dreams?" asked Ron.

"That's right, he did. In his dream, 'the sun and moon and eleven stars made obeisance (bowed down) to him.' I believe that's in Genesis, chapter thirty-seven or eight."

"We talked about that three or four weeks ago in our Sunday school class. His eleven brothers thought the stars represented them bowing down to their little young brother, and if I remember," Ron said, "boy did they ever get angry."

Eugene asked, "Did the moon and sun represent Joseph's mother and father? Would they bow down to him too?"

"Our Sunday school teacher wasn't sure." Continuing the discussion, Ron said, "Eric, I think Joseph was about our age; do you think you would welcome your brother like Joseph did?"

"If Tom threw me in a hole or sold me, I wouldn't be kind to him."

Eugene adding to the conversation, said, "You know Joseph knew Jesus would want him to forgive them, so he did."

Eric said, "Well, I guess I would too, especially after years of separation."

Eugene followed with, "Jesus would want you to."

Placing large logs on the fire, they laid down on opened bedrolls and talked about going to church, doing the right thing, and forgiveness; then Eric asked, "Ron, have you ever thought about accepting Christ?"

Without hesitation, Ron answered, "I have, but I want to make sure I understand why I should."

"I felt the same way before I gave my life to Christ," Eugene said. "I like talking about the what and whys of being a Christian; sometimes it's hard for me."

Eric said, "I accepted Christ a few months ago, and I have trouble holding grudges. Will both of you remind me if you see or hear me do something I shouldn't do?"

"I will," Ron quickly answered.

Eugene followed with, "I just did."

"Thanks. Don't you think we need to talk about what it means to be a Christian?"

"Yes, we do," Ron said. "I'm thrilled we moved to this community, and I have two good friends."

They laid on their bedrolls talking, seeing the massive dark clouds that began rolling in from the northwest that masked the Big Dipper and the luminous full moon. Scintillate lightning emitted a shimmering glow all around the low dense clouds.

Sitting up, Ron said, "Reckon it will rain on us?"

"No, I don't think so," Eric replied. "See the lightning but hear no thunder means it is far away and will probably go west of us. Even, if it rains, we will be dry under this five-ounce, twelve-millimeter thick rainproof cover."

Continuing, Ron said, "If it starts raining, our fire will extinguish."

Eric said, "Don't worry about it Ron, we'll be okay."

"If the fire goes out, won't animals smell our break-fast food and try to get it while we sleep?"

"It's right here between us, and I have my hatchet laying right by my head," Eric said. "Lay down and get some sleep; we will be okay, I promise."

Rolling on his right-side facing Ron, Eric prayed, "Lord, thanks for today, our church, Ron, Eugene, friendship, the food we eat and protect us tonight as we sleep, amen."

Sunlight crept through the treetops as the campers awoke. As the three dressed, Eric placed more wood on the still hot coals, Ron prepared to cook eggs in the old cast-iron skillet given to Eric by his grandfather. As each enjoyed their two-egg sand-wich, topped with cheese and a slice of sweet white onion, they reviewed earlier plans of exploring the cave. They assembled the gear: four hundred feet of baler twine Eric had cut from a five-thousand-foot roll, gloves, walking sticks, a small wire-bound memo book with a sharp pencil inserted in the wire spiral, a metal tent peg, and the trusted all-steel hatchet.

At the cave's entrance, Ron said, "Eric, did you know Kentucky's Mammoth Cave National Park was established in 1941 and is the home of the longest cave system known in the world with 390 miles of passageways?"

"Dad read us an article in the *Courier-Journal* about how large that cave is," Eric said, as he drove the metal tent peg deep into the ground. "Do you think we'll find any stalagmites or stalactites in this one?"

"Maybe," Ron said. "Eric, don't you think we should double-tie the string to the peg to make sure it won't come off? You know we'll have to keep it taut?"

Eugene said, "That's a smart idea."

Unwinding the string as they moved farther into the cave, Eric stopped and said, "Mom asked me if I needed a flashlight and I told her no because the moon was so bright. I forgot we would be in a cave. We don't have anything to make a torch."

"How about using this flashlight?" Ron said, pulling it out of his pocket. "I know you told me we wouldn't need one, but I brought one anyway."

Eugene said, "I have one too, but the batteries are a little weak."

As they began shining the lights on the interior walls, Eric said, "Good for you; let's move over to that narrow passage. It looks like a hallway, maybe it's leading to a large room full of gold."

Ignoring the gold remark, Ron asked, "What about that opening over there?" He pointed to a small round opening about two feet above the cave's floor.

Discussing the possibilities of both, they chose to explore the broader opening. Ron led the group. As Eric unrolled the string, Eugene followed. After a few more feet into the cave, the passage became narrower, but its height was still a good seven feet. Moving around a sharp curve, they came upon another large, man-sized opening.

"Which way should we go?"

"Ron let's keep going to the left."

"Are you still unrolling the string?" Ron asked.

"Yes, I have unrolled about half of it," Eric answered.

They were quiet as they crept along the passage, going deeper and deeper into the hole, farther and farther away from sunlight; it became darker and darker as the flashlights dimmed, and suddenly, Ron had no light. Ron flipped the switch on and off several times, shook it until it rattled, then bumped it on the wall. The little beam of Eugene's light reduced its power to a flicking glimmer, and finally, it too yielded to overuse. It was dark, thick black darkness; one could not see his hand. It was a blackness that shrouded your whole body.

Eric whispered, "Ron, I can't see."

"I know. I can't either," the answer came back faintly.

Eric said, "I'm not holding the string anymore."

Eugene asked, "When did you come to the end of it?"

"I don't know. I guess I was looking at the rock formation and forgot about it. I don't remember coming to an end or dropping it. Have we made any turns?" Eric asked.

"Yes, we made one sharp turn. We also passed an opening leading off to the right, and as we go back to the entrance, we could get sidetracked into it, instead of the way we came in."

How were they to get out without the string? They decided to turn around and keep the right hand on the wall until reaching the first opening, then feel for the line on the floor. This system worked, and within minutes the trio stood in the entrance. They welcomed the luminous rays of the sun that radiated through the pine trees around the campsite.

"Boy isn't the sunshine beautiful," Ron blurted out.

"Undeniable," Eugene added.

"Indubitably, my friends," Eric exclaimed.

"Irrefutably," Ron said, as they moved toward camp, Ron in the middle with one arm resting on each of his shoulders—a triad comradeship continued to grow.

Three exultant teenagers broke camp then navigated upstream through thickets, across sandbars, around the swimming hole, by the walnut trees, and finally, they arrived at the concrete road culvert. Climbing the bank, Eric paused momentarily at the guard-rail and said, "Could either of you help me repair Papaw's chicken fence?"

"I can help."

"Me too. When do you want to do it?" questioned Eugene.

"How about in the morning?"

Eugene said, "I can help."

Ron said, "Me too. What time?"

"Okay, how about nine?" Eric answered. "I'll meet you at the creek."

He started up the road, rehearsing in his mind the cave and camping experiences. Dropping his backpack and walking stick on the back porch, he entered the kitchen where his mother was preparing dinner. Turning, she said, "Well, the spelunker made it home."

The Christmas break over, the spring term progressed quickly with only one notable occurrence, the sundry of amicable interactions continued to deepen.

CHAPTER 7

DAD'S BROKEN ARM/ MAKING SORGHUM

IN MID-AUGUST, PREPARATION FOR harvesting tobacco began. Tobacco, garden, and other field plants produce basal growth at the base of each leaf. These "suckers" sap nutrients from the leaf and the stalk. Removing them allows the nutrients to mature and ripen the plant. Mature thick tobacco leaves saved will produce more weight and more weight sold generates more income. The federal government controlled this cultivated crop. Each year Federal agents measured for precise acreage before transplanting, and sometimes after the tobacco started growing. When using too much acreage, a farmer paid a fine, or he had to cut down the plants on the excess land or in rare cases, both; he had to spend money out of his pocket, and then he had to cut down his excess plants. The farmer could produce as much weight as he could on the allotted land. This allotment did not limit the width between rows, but just the amount of acreage. This incentive created an intense effort to use all recommendations made by the University of Kentucky Department of Agriculture: soil testing, proper fertilization, leaves saved, and correct curing, which increased the quality and the total weight of tobacco sold.

During the three weeks between suckering the tobacco and cutting it, Eric had to scatter five-foot-long white oak sticks in each baulk. Eric despised this job. As he dropped them end-to-end from a bundle of fifty carried on his shoulder, loose dirt, leaves, insects, and other debris fell into his shirt. He endured biting black angry ants crawling beneath his shirt. Spider bites were dangerous. The sting of a "packsaddle" worm hurt. With both hands dispensing the sticks, relief from the bites came only after distribution of the bundle or coming to the end of the row. Dislodged sticks on his shoulder often pinched his ears and neck.

The Brays started to cut tobacco in late August. Eric started in the first row, Tom in the second, and Dad in the third. Eric drove a stick into the ground with a wooden mallet; then he placed a sharp metal spear on the top. Cutting a six-foot stalk, he put it on the spear. Pulling the trunk down over the spear separated the fibrous stalk, allowing it to pass over the spear onto the stick. Each stick held six stalks, six inches apart. After cutting the entire patch, the tobacco was left in the field for at least three days, allowing the leaves to wilt. Valuable leaves were less likely to drop off during moving or hauling the crop to the barn. The shriveled plants also allowed more air passage between them as they hung in the barn. Doors were opened to control the moisture as soon as the morning dew dried and then closed at night. If morning moisture in the atmosphere was dry, then the doors were locked during the day and opened at night. Improper curing resulted in some leaves turning green, decreasing their value.

The day of moving the crop to the barn began with Eric and Tom carrying the full sticks of speared tobacco high above the sharp tobacco stubble to prevent damage to the ripened top leaves. After a few hours of work, their shoulders grew tired; they were exhausted by the end of the day. Taking it to the wagon, Dad loaded it carefully by propping it against a four-foot headboard. Mom pulled the wagon slowly across the field with the MT John Deere tractor, with Julie following and picking up the large savable leaves that had fallen off. Placing a hefty armload of leaves on the wagon, Julie held up her hands and shrieked, "My hands are forever ruined!" Mom could not hear the outcry, Dad smiled, Eric moved to get another load shook his head, and Tom explained what a proper hand washing could do. Julie rolled her eyes, with little aficionado of the importance for what she was doing. To retrieve more leaves, she returned to the area where Tom and Eric had carried the loaded sticks to the wagon. When in the barn, Julie had to thread these valuable bottom leaves onto an eight-inch wire and then hang them over a tobacco stick that was hung in the barn for more drying. The bottom leaves were milder and usually brought a high price when sold.

The earlier loads, Dad unloaded the wagon by handing the sticks of tobacco up to the boys. Eric hung the tobacco on the first and second tier; Tom hung it on the highest, the third tier. On the last load Dad decided to relieve Tom, so he took his position on the third tier. The wagon was about half unloaded when a tier rail that supported his left foot moved. Losing his footing, he tried desperately to grab the tier railing above. Unable to grasp it, he tumbled through the second tier still trying to halt his descent, and finally, as he passed the railing that Eric had just vacated, he was able to stabilize his tumbling body by finally grasping the tier rail and landing on his feet.

Shouting, "Dad, are you hurt?" came simultaneously from Tom, Eric, and Mom.

Julie, too concerned about her hands, did not see the fall at all.

Witnessing his slow descent to the ground, Tom said, "I don't see how you could fall from that height and land on your feet."

"Elbert, are you hurt?" Mom reiterated.

"I don't know. My right arm is numb."

Pointing to his arm, Eric said, "Dad, there is a big lump under your shirt sleeve."

Removing his long sleeve shirt revealed bleeding and a bone protruding through the skin. Mom rushed over to examine it.

After some time, she said, "Elbert, you have a broken arm. Tom, go to the house, get a clean white towel and wrap his arm, then drive your father to the hospital; he needs to see a doctor."

They left for the doctor as the sun was low on the western horizon.

"Mom, someday, when I get a car, I'm going to teach you to drive, then when someone gets hurt, you can drive them to the doctor," Eric promised. Eric was too young to drive a car; he only drove the tractor in open fields.

Mom suggested, "Eric, you take care of milking the cows, I'll feed them and the pigs. Julie, you take care of the chickens."

"I don't want to gather the eggs, I'm afraid of seeing another snake," she complained.

Mom said, "Julie, don't worry about a snake; just do it."

Eric milked three cows, took two buckets of milk to the house, and double-strained it into a ten-gallon steel can, returned to the barn, and milked three more. Returning to the steel can, he strained the milk, then placed the can in a cold-water concrete reservoir. Early the next morning, the milk would be taken to a nearby town to be made into cheese. He took one gallon of the milk to the kitchen for breakfast.

It was just before midnight when Tom and Dad returned.

Mom met them at the front door, "What did the doctor say?"

"Mom, he broke the ulna and fractured the radius. The cast must remain on for at least six weeks with no lifting and not much movement of the lower arm." Dad raised his wrapped white plaster cast arm for all to see.

News of his broken arm soon spread throughout the neighborhood. With tobacco already hanging in the barn, the only high-labor crop remaining to harvest was the sugarcane. A special called meeting at the local church scheduled work days to help the family finish harvesting the cash crop. Everyone who gathered had an obvious interest in assisting the Bray family in making sorghum. There were several steps to change this sugar holding plant into a nutritional delightful sweet. There was no persuading needed for those in attendance to volunteer for the various stages: cutting the tall stalks, removal of multi-seeded heavy heads, stripping off leaves, and hauling the crop to the boiler site. Then someone had to set the boiler pan on top of the firepit, set up the cane mill, and gather dry wood to fire the boiler. Dad promised to supervise the total operation, from the field to those golden goodies sealed in cans.

The first day of boiling the juice began just after daybreak. Three farm wagons piled high with stalks, had been pulled by mules the night before and parked next to the mill. As a mule walked in a circle turning the mill, Eric's Uncle Henry began placing two or three stalks at a time through the diagonal steel drums. The squeezed juice flowed into a bucket hanging below the mill, and eventually emptied into a large container above the boiler pan.

The Milford boys, Ron, and Larry toiled with Eric and Tom, stacking a giant pile of dry wood near the boiler. Raw juice was stored in a stainless-steel container; then it was calibrated through a spigot as it entered the big pan. The large five by ten-foot partitioned pan sat above the long firebox. Low heat cooked the juice until it thickened, strained, drained, and sealed in cans. Juice scorched changes its color, taste, and value. As it came in, it drifted across the three-inch deep, four-inch-wide partition to an opening, turned the corner, floated back to the other side, through another opening and returned to the far side until it reached a closed gate in the partition. A closed gate prevented partially cooked juice mixing with fresh raw juice. There were three sections alike in the pan. After the liquid began boiling, a perforated hand skimmer was used to remove the green foam coloration from the stalk; then the skimming was dumped into a pit about four-feet away. The inground pit was fenced to prevent accidental injury of someone falling into the hot green skimmimg. During cooking the juice was moved back and forth by a long-handled wooden spatula. When one section was cooked, stirred, and skimmed, the gate was opened, and the content floated to the next for further cooking. In each section, it was cooked more, then reskimmed and refined a little more. Reaching the final sector for inspection of clarity, quality, thickness, and color, it drained into a can. The cheesecloth laying inside the colander often became impervious; then Mom changed it. She supervised the double straining of the hot sorghum, removing all unwanted particles.

The Brays usually produced about 120 one-gallon cans. One hundred cans sold for three dollars per can and the other twenty were used for cooking or as a sweet indulgence on a hot biscuit.

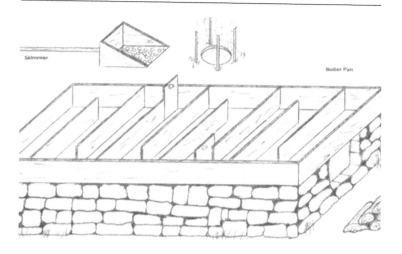

Skimmer

Boiler Pan

CHAPTER 8

EIGHTH GRADE

(1955-1956) OVER THE LAST FEW MONTHS, the trio had grown so close that Mr. Milford sought permission from Eric's and Eugene's parents to allow them to work together: one day on the Brays' farm, a day at the West's, then a day on the Milford farm. They started the summer work with two exceptions: one, each farm had to have similar needs, and two, the work had to be completed. For Eric Bray, Ron Milford, and Eugene West, the hours, days, and weeks raced by during the summer between the seventh and eighth grades.

They would start school at Eubank in one week. Larry, Ron's brother, would be entering his senior year, and Tom, Eric's brother, graduated last May, and Julie supported the title of a sophomore. This year the eighth graders moved from the two-room adjacent classroom building to the top floor of the high school building. These two rooms had large window casements, wide wooden window sills, and ligneous bookshelves beneath the windows.

Mrs. Anderson taught Language Arts: grammar, spelling, composition, and literature; she also taught Social Studies. Mr. Ray taught Math, Earth Science, and Geography. Rumors indicated Mrs. Anderson was strict but supplied proper instruction to her students, while Mr. Ray had a notorious putative, harsh, and unyielding class control. Tom informed the trio that was not always true with some kids; Mr. Ray's discipline was not the same for an athlete or a kid of a well-known family in the community. Entering the eighth grade with these rumors, Eric was concerned about his language limitations. He often thought, *will Mr. Ray make fun of me? Will I have to talk before the class? Can I become friends with any of my new classmates? Am I the only one that is challenged in enunciating many natural sounds?*

Early in the school year, a steady stream of students returned to visit Mrs. Anderson, their favorite teacher. These alumni came from a wide range of occupations: farmers, factory workers, nurses, doctors, engineers, mechanics, homemakers, lawyers, and college students. Many educators accredited her friendship, influence, and encouragement for their career choice. Mr. Ray received only a hi or a couple of hellos.

Mrs. Anderson scheduled an English test each Friday during the year. If inclement weather closed schools, the exam would be given the next Friday. She was known to return test papers the following Monday. The comprehensive examination given on Friday allowed two days for her to grade, make a written comment, and return exams. Four months of the fall term passed quickly with only one more week before Christmas break.

Ron, sitting next to Eric, leaned over as said, "You ready for this test?"

"I hope I am," Eric answered, reaching to retrieve his book and paper from the wooden window sill.

Eugene, sitting in the next row, said, "Ron, are you ready? Do you have a pencil and paper?"

With a grin, Ron replied, "I am prepared!"

"Okay students," came from the front of the room, "the paper on your desk has four short sentences: a simple sentence (declarative), a command (imperative), a question (interrogative), and an exclamatory. Choose from the words I've listed on the bottom of the page and rewrite each sentence by adding at least three adjectives or three adverbs in each sentence. Properly name each word you use as either an adjective or an adverb. Okay, go to work." She began her customary movement around the classroom; sometimes in the back, walking the aisles, in front or standing against the bookcase by the windows overlooking the Eubank Cemetery.

Eric began rewriting the sentences adding words to intensify the action or to clarify the nouns. He had to have another clean sheet of paper to finish the test, but it was in the desk below the seat. About the time Eric reached for another piece of paper, she had chosen to stand between him and the window. Unknown to him, she had placed her foot on the bottom shelf of his desk. He was hesitant to get the paper because she might accuse him of cheating. *Do not worry about that,* he thought, because she was standing right beside him. He had to have another piece of paper, so he reached below to retrieve one. Feeling around to find it, he got hold of her ankle. He quickly released it, very embarrassed. Placing her foot back on the floor, smiling she said, "Eric, you may get paper if you need it."

Ron glanced across the aisle to see Eric's discomfited appearance: red face, sweaty forehead, drawn eyebrows, and trembling hand. Eric never looked at Ron; he just got the paper and finished the test.

Eugene hadn't noticed anything.

With the exam returned, Ron whispered, "What happened?"

"I'll tell you during lunch," Eric mouthed back.

As they walked across campus to the lunchroom, which was sitting conspicuously on main street, he explained what had happened.

"You've got to be kidding us," Ron said. Ron and Eugene exploded in laughter.

"Boy was I ever embarrassed!"

"Did she jerk her foot back quick?"

"Come on, Ron; I didn't notice. I was the one with a quick movement," Eric explained. "Don't tell anyone, okay?"

"Your flirting habits are locked away for good, well, until I need them." Ron continued to joke. They included this incident in the vast accumulation of private experiences in their short and growing friendship.

Continuing the teasing, Eugene said, "Darla won't like you playing with another woman's leg."

"Darla who?"

"You know who, the Darla Aby you sit behind every day."

Ron was quick to get in on the joshing, said, "Yeah and I see you giving her paper and doing her homework."

"Come on guys; I'm just a nice person," Eric explained.

After lunch, it was time for Mr. Ray's math class. Eric quickly completed the assignment on fractions and began to fidget with a piece of paper. He folded it several times, fold over fold until it was only one-fourth of an inch wide. Eric wrapped it around the metal part of his number two new pencil. When Ron finished, and no one was watching, Eric flung the small folded paper across the aisle. It sailed across Ron's math book, landing in the next aisle on Eugene's lap. Suddenly, Mr. Ray appeared, standing right above Eric. Quickly, he grasped the hair on Eric's left temple and pulled him to his feet saying, "Young man, I don't allow this!" Laughingly, he said, "What you did is not buful!" He stood for several minutes mimicking Eric's incorrect pronunciation of other triphthong sounds before releasing his hold on Eric's hair. As he triumphantly returned to the front, he continued lecturing proper behavior, "You saw what happened to Bray; don't let this happen to you."

All the boys, except Eugene and Ron, either smiled or giggled. About half of the girls laughed, and the others expressed unbelief.

Humiliated and crestfallen, Eric sat down. He understood he did something that deserved punishment, but never had he been chastised this way. He could not decide which was worse: the pain or the embarrassment. His dad had always told him that before you misbehave, determine if you are willing to take the punishment; if caught, don't complain.

Later in the day, a basketball player did the same thing Eric had done, and the only correction he received was a verbal reprimand, "don't let me see you do that again." Ron and Eugene glanced at Eric in disbelief; they could not believe the extreme ridicule, pain, and embarrassment directed at Eric just minutes before and just a light verbal warning was given to the other student for the same behavior. What he considered unfair or one-sided treatment, hurt. Suppressed emotions awoke, animosity stirred in his heart, and seething resentment boiled up in his mind. Then Eric thought about a recent sermon on practicing forgiveness. *Should I or shouldn't I forgive old man Ray? If I forgive him,* Eric reflected, *he won't change his style of punishment, so what's the need?*

The raw feelings of hostility and resentment stayed imprisoned in the young fourteen-year-old teenager. The impetuous mien of Mr. Ray framed Eric's behavior for the entire eighth-grade year. He spoke only when called upon and never volunteered for any verbal response or blackboard work. The remembrance of this one incident would never leave Eric's memory.

Boarding the bus, Eric, Ron, and Eugene sat on the front seat. The conversation during the bus ride home included Junior, the driver, who added his opinion of Mr. Ray. He knew other challenged students to whom Mr. Ray had shown similar contempt and scornful treatment. Junior asked, "Eric, have you forgiven him?"

"No."

"You should."

Eric asked, "Why? He won't change?"

Junior continued, "Forgiveness is not about him; it's about you."

Eric answered with a high voice that showed antipathy, "I'll think about."

Ron asked, "Do you think your parents will talk to Mr. Ray?"

"No, I know what Dad will say: 'You did something wrong, got caught, and punished, end of story.' I'm going to discuss this with my grandfather; he always gives me good advice."

"I know you stay with him a lot; I want to revisit them," Ron said.

"You can help me repair the chicken fence again, if you want to."

Eugene said, "I'll help."

"Great. We'll do it next week," Eric informed them.

CHAPTER 9

THE TRIO'S TWO-DAY CAMPING TRIP

THE DIALOGUE DRIFTED AWAY FROM THE events of the day to excursions during Christmas break.

"Ron, Eugene, what are you doing for the next two weeks?"

"Let's go camping."

"I'm ready," Eugene inserted into the conversation.

Ron said, "Let's go next week."

Eric asked, "How about Monday? Can you both go?"

A double "I can," came from the pair.

As the school bus approached Ron's driveway, he said, "Can we meet tomorrow to make plans?"

"Why don't we meet by the bridge about one? It's in the center of where we all live," Eric replied.

After the agreement was made, all bade Junior farewell as they arrived at their respective homes and exited the bus. They would see him again in January.

The Bray's Friday evening meal was different now that Tom was gone—no lengthy oration on good grades or new girls. Julie assumed his place at the end of the table; she discussed the latest fashion, dreadful boys, and the latest hairstyles. As the meal progressed, Eric considered telling them about the incidents with Mrs. Anderson's ankle and Mr. Ray's chastisement. *I know what Dad will say*, he thought, *so I will not tell about either event.* Going to bed after supper, he lay on his back staring at the ceiling. His soul was troubled. Eric had an uncomfortable feeling about Mr. Ray. *How can I become free of it?* Something spoke to him, "Ask, and it will be given you" Matthew 7:7, (KJV). As he lay with his hands across his stomach he thought, *what will be given?* Nothing came to his mind. Then a profound sense arose within him, "What about 'ask'?" *Maybe I should pray,* he thought; so, he began praying. "Jesus, what can I do? Lord, give me an understanding of why I feel so much resentment toward Mr. Ray, forgive me, Lord, for doing something in class that I should not have done, and Lord, lift this burden from my heart." As he drifted off to sleep, he realized his soul was at rest, the burden gone, at least for now Matthew 11:29-30, (KJV).

Eric asked for permission to camp with his close friends. Eric's dad knew the importance of 1 Corinthians 15:33 (NIV), which states, "Bad company corrupts good character," so his parents consensually agreed that his ascertained friendship with Ron and Eugene was a posit. He could go for two days. Ron and Eugene respected their parents, worked hard, used no foul language, and they attended church services.

Only five of the thirteen cows were now producing milk, the other eight were dry and would have calves in the spring. A "dry cow" is the term used to describe a cow that has stopped giving milk two months before giving birth; it's nature's way of allowing the cow to remain healthy and still have a vigorous offspring.

Julie even agreed to gather the eggs while Eric was gone; it was too cold for snakes.

Saturday at one o'clock, Eric, Ron, and Eugene met at the bridge to complete plans for the upcoming camping trip. Eric started the conversation, "Let's ask our parents if we can stay two nights."

Both Ron and Eugene thought they could.

Eric asked, "Okay, do we need a tent?"

"I have a tent that sleeps four, but I like making our shelter like we did the last time we camped," answered Ron. "We cannot enjoy the beautiful moon and stars enclosed in a tent."

Eugene approved with a nod of his head and said, "I like waking up and seeing the stars."

"Okay, Ron and I will bring our cooking pots and pan," Eric replied. "Ron, tell us what else we might need."

"We'll need the waterproof fabric for the shelter, sleeping bags, quarter-inch nylon rope, four tent pegs, an ax, hunting knives, a long string, flashlights, walking sticks, and food."

Eugene quickly added, "I can bring canned pork sage sausage and eggs."

Finalizing the list of supplies needed for a successful camping trip, they left for home and promised to see each other in church.

The next morning, the preacher's enthusiastic sermon came from John 10:10 (KJV), where Jesus said, "I am come that they may have life, and have it more abundantly." The teenagers interpreted a "full life" as one with a lot of excitement, exploring, and having fun; they did not understand that along the road of Christian service that a "full life" also included forgiveness and the abundance of God's grace.

Eric, Ron, and Eugene were two seats in front of Uncle Boyd, when Ron whispered, "Reckon he will stand up during the sermon?"

They all smiled. Eric had not told them of his part in Uncle Boyd's sudden jumping to his feet during a sermon months ago; they had only heard of his sudden standing.

With Monday morning chores done, Eric brought in extra wood, and shelled two buckets of yellow corn for the chickens; he didn't see the resident black-snake in the crib. He then set two buckets of corn by the pigpen and made sure the water reservoir in the large standby cookstove in the kitchen was full. His mom used it for heat in the winter and canning in the summer instead of the new electric stove across the room.

Gathering his backpack, walking stick, and flash-light, Eric met Ron and Eugene at the road cul-vert. Double checking flashlights, batteries, food, matches, sleeping bags, ropes, string, and walking sticks, the trio slipped over the grassy bank and began their journey. As they moved from gravel bar to gravel bar, jumped from the creek to solid ground on the bank, Ron pointed to traces left by animals: a track, a rabbit's concealed lair, or a hummingbird's spider-silk reinforced nest.

When the trio approached the hazelnut thicket hiding the swimming hole, Ron described what he and Eric had seen on their first camping trip. They paused at the fallen tree after passing the deep pool and going around the wild blackberry grove.

Pointing to the dense thicket on the left, Eric said, "Look at the labyrinth of paths coming from every direction."

Eugene said, "They are crisscrossing too. What kind of animals use these trails?"

"Last year, when Eric and I camped by ourselves, we saw a raccoon nursery and an opossum family," Ron answered.

"What is a raccoon nursery?"

"It's a mother raccoon training her babies where to go and what to eat," Eric explained.

Moving downstream, they came to the waterfall. The trio sat on the creek bank watching the mist as it floated upward and finally disappeared into the air. "There is not much roar, is there?"

Eric asked, "Eugene, now why would you say that?"

"Well, the preacher mentioned King David referring to the 'roar of the waterfalls' in one of the king's songs" Psalm 42:7, (NIV).

"You know King David loved God's nature master-pieces, one being the waterfalls," Eric said. "So maybe the waterfall he was talking about was high and wide."

"This waterfall is beautiful, isn't it?"

After some discussion about waterfalls, they moved downstream to the plateau just north of the cave. They set up camp across from the cliff. The rocks were still around the fire ring, the forked limbs still in place to support the pole, the steel tent peg was still in the ground, and even the string was tied to it—just the way it was when they broke camp on the previous trip.

The trio gathered firewood, strung ropes between four large pine trees, placed rainproof fabric in place, arranged sleeping bags, set the steel bucket holding eggs and the canned sausage in the stream; then they went to the cave entrance.

Going a few feet into the cave, Eric turned and said, "Since we don't have a lot of time before it gets dark, let's see if we can get through that small hole."

As light illuminated the entrance, it exposed a twelve-foot-long passageway that would be a tight squeeze for any of the trio. Eugene said as he leaned over, peering into the opening, "There is a larger cavity beyond the twelve-feet, and I believe I hear water either running or dripping."

"Okay, I'll go first," Eric said. "Tie this rope to my feet, and if I get stuck, you can help me move backward."

Climbing into the narrow passage, he began wiggling forward using his elbows, and soon he peered into a large cavernous room, high enough to stand upright. Untying the rope and sliding into the sizeable space, Eric motioned the others to follow. "It is not as narrow as I thought it would be."

When all three stood in the room, three flashlights illuminated the whole chamber.

"Do you think we should save one light? If we overuse them, we will have one to help us find our way out?" questioned Eugene.

"That is a smart idea," Ron said, "I brought extra batteries if we need them."

As the trio carefully surveyed the spacious chamber, water slowly dripped from the ceiling onto the floor, disappearing into a large crack. As the two flashlights passed over the ceiling surface and gradually descended along the opposite wall, Eric's back became active again. Chills started in his lower back radiating up his spine, across his shoulders and ending in the upper arms. Before one ended, another began. To shake off this eerie feeling, he shook his shoulders.

Eugene asked, "Eric, is something wrong?"

"No, why do you ask?"

"I thought you were shrugging your shoulders like something was wrong."

"Yeah, I just had chills going up my back and across the shoulders," Eric said. "It is a little unnerving in here, isn't it?"

"Spooky is the word," suggested Ron.

As the bright light shifted around the room, it passed over what appeared to be a level surface about four feet above the floor. As the trio moved across the floor, they realized the outer raised lip concealed a full, fifteen-inch-wide smooth shelf. As the three stood alongside the rim, Ron moved the light to his left. Instantly, the trio rushed to the small opening that led to the outside.

Eric hurriedly suggested, "I came in first, I'll go out first."

"I am the youngest, so I'll go first!" exclaimed Eugene. He was three months younger than either Eric or Ron.

Before either knew it, Ron was through, Eugene followed, and Eric very close behind. They soon stood under the overhang, breathing hard and looking at the others' colorless faces. The flashlights quivering in their hands were still on in the late afternoon sunlight.

Eric was the first to speak, "What did you see on that shelf?"

Eugene was slow to respond. "I think it was a cap or maybe a hat of some kind."

Ron was bent over clasping his knees with both hands, breathing rapidly, still unable to speak. Finally standing erect, his eyes and facial countenance told everything. With a trembling squeaky voice, he said, "What was that?"

The camp talk was more of a teenager chitter-chatter than a recognizable problem-solving conversation. It was like:

"It was a cap."

"No, it was a hat."

"It moved."

"No, it did not move."

"Did you see that bone under it?"

"There was no bone."

"Boy, you were scared."

"You were too."

"Okay, okay, let us calm down," Eric suggested. "We will build a fire, eat our supper, and talk about what we saw, okay?"

Sitting in front of the campfire with legs crossed, eating hot dogs with pork and beans from plates on their laps, a candid discussion of the cave incident began.

Eric said, "The only thing I saw on that shelf was a cap."

"I didn't look at it for very long, but I think it had a brim on two sides," Ron offered.

"I think it was just a cap, and the brim you thought you saw was a bone, maybe even a small human bone," Eugene proposed.

"A bone? A human bone, that's ridiculous. It was just a cap," Eric inserted. "We all saw something different; I saw only a cap, Ron saw a hat with a brim, and Eugene saw a cap with a bone sticking out one side."

It's apparent the teenagers had suddenly developed active anxieties; could they harness them into constructive controlled imagination?

"What are we going to do?" Ron asked.

"We'll go back in the morning to see what it is," Eugene said. "Ron, you go in first."

"Why me?"

"Well, you were the first one back through the narrow passage to the outer chamber, so I thought you would want to go in first this time," suggested a smiling Eugene.

"I agree," grinned Eric.

"I knew you would have the same idea."

"It is probably just a hat of some kind, so let us not get scared. All three will go back in and see just what it is, okay?" informed Eric.

Eugene asked, "How do you think it got there?"

"Maybe someone just laid it there," Ron said.

"Maybe Mr. Culhwich left it there."

"Oh, come on Eric, I thought he was dead," Ron nervously said.

"Well, maybe his ghost put it there."

Eugene eager to get in the ambiguous discussion said, "Maybe he was in the chamber with us and just walked over and put it there right in front of us."

The trio laughed tensely.

Eric piled extra wood on the campfire. The trio climbed into their sleeping bags amid a flurry of suggestions, opinions, speculations, and conjectures, lasting far past midnight. The raccoon nursery feeding in the creek just a few feet north of the camp heard three soft susurrus conversations, then only two, and finally one, then only snoring. As the little nocturnal family moved downstream, they shuffled through the dirty plates and silverware just below the boy's feet. The clanging of metal did not awake the trio.

Neither Ron nor Eugene ever noticed Eric's slight mispronunciation while camping, at school or in private discussions. Eric's friendship with these two very close and trusted inseparable buddies strengthened his self-esteem. He deeply valued this companionship. It reminded him of Jonathan and

David's alliance described in 1 Samuel 20:42 (NIV) where they "swore friendship with each other in the name of the Lord."

Early the next morning as the sun peeped over the trees, the boys began to awaken. Ron quickly dressed, shored up the campfire, and had six eggs cooking before the others awoke.

Eugene sat up, stretched, yawned, and said, "Boy, that smells good, but I don't smell sausage."

"You told us last night that it was fully cooked and the only thing we had to do was to heat it. I will heat the sausage balls after I cook the eggs."

The West family butchered three or four hogs every fall; they cooked and canned the sage flavored sausage balls. As the hot rendered lard was poured into the jar filled with cooked sausage balls, it cooled, and formed a vacuum, sealing the lid. It provided a good source of protein for the West family.

"Did anyone have bad dreams last night?" quizzed Eric.

"Nope," came from both.

The trio finished eating, cleaned utensils, straightened sleeping bags, gathered necessary items, and started toward the cave. In the frontal chamber, they approached the long narrow passageway that led to the inner-chamber with the shelf.

"Who wants to go first?" Eric asked.

"I don't," Eugene quickly answered.

"Me neither," Ron hurriedly replied.

"Okay, I'll go first, but I'll wait until you both get in and then we'll all examine the cap, hat, bone, or whatever we saw yesterday."

When all three were in the cave, they walked over to the shelf. Three flashlights cast a bright glow on the left side of the ledge. The hat was not there. The flashlights began shifting along the ten-foot-long shelf.

"There it is," Ron said.

The trio moved to the right, and Eugene tried to lift the hat with his walking stick. Suddenly Ron whispered, "Wait a minute, that thing was on the other end of this ledge last night."

Sighing, Eric said, "You know, I think you're right."

Eugene asked, "How did it get to this end? What is going on?"

A final examination established that it was only a baseball cap; it had no brim or bone.

Eric asked, "It looks like it has been worn a lot, but how could it have gotten here, and what moved it last night?"

"Leave the cap, let's see what else might be in here," Ron suggested.

As three lights illuminated the large chamber, Eugene pointed to the large shadow on the far side. A massive pillar-like vertical wall cast a shadow that was unnoticed last night in their short examination of the compartment. Moving to the partition, they discovered a narrow vertical aperture leading to the darkness beyond the light beams. Ron volunteered to walk down to the opening and check how far it went and if it had turns or other fissures. As he cautiously moved sideways between the rock walls, Eric and Eugene stood silently, wondering what he might find.

Eric finally asked, "Ron, what have you found?"

"It is pretty narrow here. I just passed a small hole, and it looks like it might go into a large cavity," Ron announced. Retracing his steps, he soon stood beside them. "It leads nowhere."

There was no more interest in this part of the cave, so they decided to crawl back through to the frontal chamber and explore the other hallway. The trio moved along the narrow passageway and around the bend of smooth limestone rock. As they continued along the rocky corridor, it became narrower and the floor more inclined; it would lead them deeper and deeper into the cave.

Eugene asked, "See anything?"

"It looks like there might be another large chamber just a few more feet," Eric answered.

Entering the sizeable bedroom-sized rock cavity, the ceiling, walls, and the floor was a dazzling sight for the young adventurous teenagers. Beautiful stalactites hung in the middle of the ceiling and small stalagmites rose up along the center of the floor. Water was running in a small narrow stream from wall to wall. It seemed to be unnoticed as it rippled slowly across to the other side, disappearing into a large crevice. The floor was flat on each side of the waterway except near the stalagmites. Ron began poking his walking stick into the six-inch deep water.

"What are you doing?" questioned Eugene.

"It looks shallow, but there might be a large hole we can't see," he responded. He continued along the water until it disappeared into the crevice. Satisfied that no dangerous hole existed, he turned to Eric and said, "This is awesome, isn't it?"

"Irrefutable."

"Incontrovertible," Eugene added.

Ron said, "Our parents will not believe us when we tell them about this room."

Eugene suggested, "Maybe we shouldn't tell them."

Time had passed quickly in their extensive examination of the unusual formations deep underground.

Eric asked, "Who has a watch?"

"I don't," Ron said, "Why do you ask?"

"I'm hungry."

"Me too," Eugene added.

"Let's go back to camp and have lunch, talk about this room, and then we can explore the passageway leading off to the right," Eric pointed out.

As the trio sat around the fire ring, tiny puffs of smoke still curled upward from the unattended fire, then vanished. They sat talking about the cave's beauty and the indescribable magnificence of the thirty-foot waterfall encased in tall and creeping greenery. Which was the most beautiful: the waterfall they walked by earlier or the cave? The dark green ivy and the leaves of the holly bush framed the yellowish honeysuckle leaf amid small ferns growing on the rock wall. The ferns growing among the ivy were brilliant green, some had an orange-yellowish leaf, while others had variegated stems and leaves. It was easy to think the plants were moving as the mist floated upward through the vegetation. If the stalactites and stalagmites were in the open with greenery and a tinge of color, its beauty would marvel the waterfall's splendor.

Eric suggested exploring the peripheries of the hundred acres of second-growth timber just behind the campsite for contorted saplings. A plaudit quickly came from Ron and Eugene.

CHAPTER 10

A NEIGHBOR'S MOONSHINE STILL

AFTER LUNCH, THE TRIO MOVED ALONG the edge of the young timber next to the creek. The area had been clear-cut ten years ago. Clear-cut logging is a forestry/logging practice in which most or all trees in an area are uniformly cut down. Clear-cutting allowed the logger to cut all the trees regardless of size, on a given track of timber, even cutting limbs into firewood. It left only small branches to decay, stumps to decompose, and young saplings to grow amid wild vegetation of climbing vines, blackberry briars, hazelnut thickets, thorny multiflora rose, and an assortment of other wild undergrowth. Moving single file through this ten-year tangled growth was slow and difficult. Turning away from the creek, they walked toward an extensive log ridden gulley looking for a desired twisted and contorted sapling.

"Over here is one," Ron said, pointing to a small spotted tree camouflaged in vines and briars.

"That is a little big, but it will do. Ron, if you want it, we will cut it down."

He answered, "I want it. What kind of tree is it?"

Eric said, "I believe it's a sycamore."

After cutting the little tree to the proper length, stripping off the vines and inspecting it, Ron had a new contorted walking stick. Going several hundred feet deeper into the groves' tangled undergrowth, they came to a ravine with a small sloping meadow. At the bottom of the slope, a crystal-clear stream trickled along a shallow ditch before disappearing beneath a bolder. Scouting the boundaries unsuccessfully for another tree, the teenagers moved to the southern rim of the gully. Scrambling several feet up the bare incline, Eugene hollered, "Wait a minute, look at these rocks!"

Ron stopped climbing and ask, "What kind of rocks are they?"

Eugene answered, "It's flint."

"Maybe we can find some arrowheads," Eric said. "Let's look for a while; it's going to get dark in about thirty-five minutes so we'll have to start back to camp soon."

Eugene stopped halfway up the bank and said, "What is that funny odor?"

"I smell it too," Eric said.

Ron suggested, "Maybe it is coming from one of these plants we're walking through."

Searching the exposed bank for several minutes, they found no valuable early American relic. No one mentioned the odd smell again. The trio arrived back at camp and discussed what they were going to do the next morning. Eric and Ron had to be home by one, Wednesday afternoon, so they decided to visit the gully the following day to search for artic facts, specifically arrowheads and stone axes. They would explore the cave on the next camping trip.

The following day, after a hearty breakfast, the triad began searching the embankment again. Eric started to pull the tangled growth away from a small area near the little brook when he suddenly yelled, "Look what I found!" He had uncovered an arrowhead in pristine condition.

The duo converged on the site; they hurriedly helped Eric remove the undergrowth around the bushes. A few minutes later, Ron exclaimed, "Look what I found." He had found an almost perfect stone ax.

After going a short distance into the underbrush and finding no other relics; they came upon a well-used trail. Looking down the trail, Eric said, "It goes to the water in the ravine." Looking uphill along the path, he continued, "Let's see where else it goes."

Eugene asked, "What do you suppose made this trail: deer, raccoons, or what?"

"There are no deer or raccoon tracks; it's beaten down from shoes," Ron answered. He continued, "I smell that odd smell again."

The trio made their way up the trail, sometimes hunching down to go through a tunnel of tangled vines woven in the thick brush overhead. The path began to be more open with fewer vines among the thicket. The odd smell became stronger as they came nearer to the origin. The odor wafted on the slight breeze. Eric stopped, held up his hands and whispered, "I don't like that smell, I've smelled that same odor many times while I was roaming over the woods across the road; sometimes it was stronger than it is today."

At once, Ron and Eugene heeded the warning by Eric. Eugene softly asked, "What is producing that smell?"

Quickly moving ahead, Eric motioned the other two to follow. About one hundred feet up the trail and around a curve, the trio came upon a large pot set on stones. There was charred wood under the vessel; apparently, a fire had been built under it. A metal coiled copper tubing hung from the top; it dropped downward, almost to the ground. The pot sat in the middle of a ten-foot square beaten flat area and a path that led uphill from it.

Eric, still whispering, said, "Let's get out of here."

Eric led the others silently down the path beyond where they had entered the trail. The trail ended at a large deep pool in the ravine. Jumping over the water into the clearing, they began talking.

Ron asked, "Eric, were you scared? What was that?"

"Was someone camping up there?" Eugene asked.

"I wasn't scared. That was a moonshine still, and you don't fool around with moonshiners," Eric responded. "We'll talk about it on the way back to camp."

Ron asked, "Was that odd smell, moonshine?"

"Yes, it had probably been spilled on the ground," Eric answered. "I was hunting in this area last year and saw another still about a mile farther into the woods. I never told anyone because if Dad had known about it, he would not have let me hunt."

Eugene asked, "Should we tell about finding the still?"

Eric said, "I don't think we should."

"I have a question," Ron announced, "I thought it took corn and sugar to make moonshine."

"You're right." Eric added, "Here is the way Uncle Esau explained the process: field corn is ground into cornmeal, sugar mixed with it, and then the mixture is cooked. At some point, yeast is added to the mixture."

Eugene wanted in on the conversation, said, "We only saw that large pot with the coiled copper tubing. Where was the corn?"

Eric, trying to recall what Uncle Esau had told him about this process, scratched his head and said,

"After cooking, the mixture ferments, then it becomes a liquid; that liquid is brought up here and turned into alcohol."

Eugene still wanted to know, said, "But where is the corn?"

Eric explained, "They do that at home and feed the fermented grain to the hogs or chickens. They only have to carry the liquid to the still for the distilling process."

Eugene followed with, "It's illegal to make shine, but not fermenting cornmeal, right?"

"I suppose," Eric answered.

Discovery of a real still, not the cap that was moved during the night, was the focal point of discussion all the way back to camp. Breaking camp and on their way home, they planned another camping trip to explore the cave's passage that led to the right of the frontal chamber and take a second look at the baseball cap. It was still a mystery of how or what moved the cap.

In the next three months of school, the trio speculated on what had moved the cap; even the bus driver, Junior, had an opinion. No one mentioned the moonshine still.

Eric, Ron, and Eugene had only a few more weeks of school to finish the eighth grade. Without another important phenomenon, they just had a collective pack of abjuration of Mr. Ray's unfair treatment of students.

CHAPTER 11

DANGEROUS STORM

ON THE LAST DAY OF SCHOOL IN LATE May, as the Brays boarded the old bus, Junior Brooks, the driver, pointed to the heavy-laden clouds in the west and said, "I hope we get to school before those rain clouds turn loose."

"They do look bad," Eric said. "What if it starts raining just before we get to Buck Creek?"

"I can't let you kids stay on the bus as I drive across. That bridge is too dangerous. If it is a light rain, you can hurry across the bridge, then I will pick you up on the other side. If the storm hits about the time we get to the bridge, everyone will have to stay on the bus and wait until it passes."

For the next thirty minutes, the bus traveled the twisted narrow gravel roads, picking up twenty-three students. As they continued toward the bridge, the clouds hung lower than earlier, and the wind increased. Coming down the last hill to the bottomland along the creek, it began to rain hard. Driving the last mile along the alluvial, torrents of water began to beat against the windows. Junior pulled up to the bridge and stopped, leaving the engine running.

Junior calmly said, "We'll have to wait until the storm stops."

Fearing for their safety, Junior moved students away from the three loose-fitted and cracked windows. Large hail began pelting the right side of the yellow student transport. The storm had dropped into the valley between the hills and raced southward, straight toward the bus parked on the roadway, fifteen feet above the valley floor. Only a few three-year-old trees, bushes, and briers growing on the bank stood between the storm and Junior's precious cargo. The bank growth offered no protection. Junior sat patiently, trying to keep the children calm, hoping the storm would soon pass. The wind howled, the downpour increased, and the bus shook.

Suddenly Junior shouted, "Get your feet and legs out of the aisle! I'm going to back up; the left mirror is gone." Ramming the gearshift into reverse, and as the engine roared to life, he turned in his seat to guide the bus backward looking through the window in the back-escape door. With the engine at full throttle, the students braced for a violent lurch backward; the bus didn't move. It sat there shaking in the storm with torrents of driving rain beating against the side. Lightning danced all around the heavy clouds, flashes of charged particles plummeted to the ground. Everyone was frightened, and some of the girls cried. As wind threatened to roll the bus off the high roadway, Junior reengaged the gearshift, as he quickly released the clutch, the student transport lurched backward. He guided the jitney out of the direct path of the storm and stopped behind a hill over a half-mile from the creek. They sat there for an hour with Junior reassuring everyone they were safe; the dangerous storm finally passed. As the thunder, lightning, and rain moved south, away from the roadway, Junior pulled the bus back to the bridge and unloaded the students as if nothing exciting had happened. He then pulled across the squeaky boards, stopped, opened the door, politely smiled, and said, "All aboard."

After lunch, the student body gathered in the gym for a pleasant farewell and was encouraged to read during the summer vacation. The principal, Mr. Halbright, announced that the school library would be open from eight to four on the second and fourth Fridays of each month. On the way to the bus, Eric, Ron, and Eugene talked about camping, spelunking, cap moving, and waterfalls. No one mentioned the moonshine still because they had taken a pledge not to reveal what they had seen in the woods.

Limbs, leaves, and other debris still cluttered the road at Buck Creek. The rusty white sign that had stood boldly in front of the bridge warning travelers, "Two-ton limit," was gone.

On the way home, the freshmen trio planned a lengthy camping trip.

During supper that evening, Mom announced that Tom would not be home for the summer because he had taken a job in another city. Surprisingly, Julie, now a high school junior, asked Mom to give her some sewing lessons. She had signed up for Home Economics. Just before he left the table, Eric nonchalantly mentioned that Ron and Eugene wanted to go camping next week. "Dad, do you suppose I could take them sometime?"

"When?" he asked.

"Anytime you don't need me," Eric answered.

"Well, I suppose I can do without you this Thursday, Friday, and Saturday." He continued, "The garden is planted and the tobacco set, but Monday morning we must pick strawberries."

"Thanks, Dad. I'll get extra corn for the chickens, extra feed for the cows, corn, and water for the pigs."

"Julie can help milk."

"Dad, you've got to be kidding me!" She shrieked. "What about my hands, my fingernails?"

"Then you can feed the chickens, gather the eggs, and feed the pigs."

Julie, the high school junior, turned on Eric with tight lips, drawn eyebrows making wrinkles in her smooth forehead, and a scornful glare in her eyes fixated on Eric. She was incredulous at Dad's request.

"Mom!" she yelled.

"If Dad wants you to do all that, then just do it."

Dad just sat there, relishing in teasing his only daughter. He was not known to be part of any silliness. This was not one of Dad's proclivities.

"Julie, I was jesting you," he said. "Doing a few chores won't hurt you. All the cows but three have calves, so I'll do the milking, and I'll feed the pigs."

"Dad, I won't go if it will cause a problem," Eric said, without looking in Julie's direction. The waves of contempt still flowed across the room.

"No son, you go camping. Your friendship with those two boys is important. Remember how important the friendship between King David and Jonathan was. First Samuel 20:42 (NIV) says it lasted a lifetime for both. Talk to your friends about becoming a Christian."

"Eugene is already a Christian, and I think Ron is almost ready to accept Christ and be baptized."

During the weekend and the days before Thursday morning, Eric never mentioned camping around Julie. She was still steaming about the suggestion of milking the foul, stinking cows.

After church services on Sunday, Ron invited Eric and Eugene to dinner. The three often ate in the Milford home, and in the Bray's and the West's. The teenagers were inseparable. After eating, the trio had no reluctance to the appeal of the soft, thick grass in the orchard. The triad lay on their backs, legs pulled back, and one leg laid on the other knee. A few small cotton-ball clouds floated languidly under a beautiful azure sky. Having a full stomach, happiness, comradeship, a warm afternoon underneath trees filled with melodies of songbirds, soon, they all fell asleep. The trio awoke and completed plans for camping; they would meet at the concrete culvert Thursday morning about nine, and each would bring his part of the food and other items needed for the campout.

CHAPTER 12

A THREE-DAY CAMPING TRIP

FINALLY, AT NINE O'CLOCK ON THURSDAY morning, the boys met at the culvert with full backpacks and walking sticks, two contorted and Eugene's converted white oak tobacco stick.

Eric said, "Okay, let's check our important supplies."

"Bible, walking sticks."

"Here, here," came with laughter.

As the laughter decreased, Eugene asked, "Hey, when are we going to look for a twisted stick for me?"

Did the love for each other or the desire to have a contorted, crooked, and knotty sapling reveal something about the threesome? Did having a woody companion provide comfort, pity, empathy, compassion, kindness, or understanding? Did psychological constraints at birth plea for peculiar similarities? Is there a resemblance, a parallel, or did the unthoughtful verbal comments reist or overwhelm the natural development of a person? Are all children affected the same way? How was Eugene's life? Did he have problems? If so, what kind of problems? Were they like Ron's or Eric's?

Ron answered, "Eugene, we'll try to find one before we come home."

Perambulating along the familiar Barney Branch, they passed the swimming hole, the labyrinth trails at the hazelnut and brier thicket, around the fallen rotting oak log, and the beautiful waterfall, until they came to the camping plateau. Laying the twelve-by-twelve fabric near the stream's bank, they arranged the sleeping bags, then began to eat their sandwiches.

Ron, still chewing his ham sandwich, spoke first, "What should we do first? Explore the cave or find the still?"

"The still," Eugene answered. He continued, "We can look for my contorted walking stick, see if we can find an arrowhead, then see the still."

"That's a clever idea," Eric said. He continued, "We can explore the cave after dark, but we'll need the sunshine to get through that undergrowth thicket."

Ron added, "And the overgrowth." Vines had grown to the treetops and along limbs to other trees; it was a real jungle of wild vegetation.

The three left for the ravine, hunting knives fastened to their belts, walking sticks in hand, and one steel hatchet. They moved slowly through the tangle of vines, briers, saplings, rotting limbs, and other wild vegetation. Their earlier trip through this same section was not noticeable. Plant life had utterly retaken it. Finally coming to the opening around the ravine, they at once began searching for Indian relics. Eugene was more intense in his search that the others. He wanted to find a relic. Moving to the top of the incline, he found a foot-high boulder covered by vines. Pulling the vines away from the boulder exposed a round depression. It was three inches wide and two inches deep. The rock had a perfectly hollowed-out hole in the top. When he realized what he had found, he summoned Eric and Ron. He yelled, "Come to see what I've found."

They rushed to the top of the incline wanting to see the discovery. Ron was first coming to the top of the slope. He fell to his knees, asking, "What is it?"

Eric, close behind Ron, fell on his knees and began removing the vegetation, and said, "I've never seen anything like it. What do you suppose it is?"

The trio continued to remove the wild growth amid a lot of supposing from Eric and Ron. Eugene remained silent but eagerly cleared the "relic find" until the whole stone was visible.

He quietly said, "I know what it is."

"What is it?"

"Eric, it is a 'Mortar Bowl,'" Eugene spoke as one with authority on Indian relics.

Ron asked, "What in the world is a 'Mortar Bowl'?"

"It is a rounded-out depression in a large rock; some rocks can be handheld; grain is put into the hole to be ground into powder."

Ron said, "Boy, this is neat. This rock looks heavy. How are we going to take it home?"

Now all three were on their knees around the rock, removing the stuck-on leaves.

Eugene quickly said, "Okay, let's look for the 'club.'"

Ron asked, "You mean the contorted walking stick?"

"No, I should have said a 'Pestle.' It's a blunt club-shaped stone with a rounded end that fits into this depression to crush or grind things," Eugene added.

The trio began stripping away growth for four feet around the rock. Finding nothing, they sat down, considering what to do next. Eric turned to Eugene and said, "Boy, you sure know a lot about Indian relics. Did you learn this in school?"

"Well, I did some research for a paper I had to write as an assignment for Mrs. Anderson. I read a library book about Indian artifacts. Dad loves history so much he read the whole book before I had to return it."

Ron said, "My dad never reads anything I bring home from school, except notes from the teacher and my report card."

Eric added, "About the only things my dad reads are the *Courier-Journal*, the Bible, and a lot of Bible tracts."

Eugene said, "Maybe they're too busy or too tired from farm work to sit and read."

Sitting there for some time, disappointed because they found nothing, they finally decided to locate the still. The trio moved through the tangled mess, found the beaten-down path, moved toward the opening, and there it sat on the rock foundation. Examining the burned fire logs under it, they concluded that the still had not been used since the earlier discovery. Going around the still, a half-hidden path going northward through the woods became noticeable. Leaving so quickly before, they had not followed it. Eric assumed it would lead to the county road adjacent to the timber.

Feeling uncomfortable around the still, Eric suggested, "Let's take another way back to camp; maybe we can find another twisted sapling for Eugene."

"I'll lead the way," Ron eagerly declared, as he moved away from the still.

The other two hurriedly followed. Why did Eric and Ron want Eugene to have a walking stick like the ones they had? It is just a simple worthless stick. It held memories for Eric of his favorite Uncle Esau. Did the other two boys need memories tied to a cheap stick? Is it related to the meaning of teenager camaraderie, a mental phenomenon, brain coupling, or biblical teachings? Are their efforts in getting Eugene a contorted stick aimed at keeping him from coveting or was there something else? In Romans 13:9 (NIV) it says, "The commandments, 'Do not commit adultery,' 'Do not murder,' 'Do not steal,' 'Do not covet,' and whatever other commandment there may be, are summed up in this one rule: 'Love your neighbor as yourself.'" This incredible desire attests to the fact that love or a bond between people, especially teenagers, promotes self-esteem; it also strengthens character. Even though they do not understand the developing of a quality spiritual life, they are well on their way as teenagers. If they continue to walk with the Lord, He will transform their minds. The love of parents, grandparents, and the church will guide them in troublesome times.

Wedging their way through 1,100 feet of the tangled growth toward camp, Eric suddenly said, "I've found one!"

Sure enough, there stood a little one-inch sapling all entangled in gripping poison ivy and oak vines; the tree was overgrown with vines, moss, and lichens. Ron backed up a couple of steps and said, "I can't help you get that stick. I'm allergic to poison ivy."

Eric said, "I'll get it; I'm not allergic to it."

Eugene added, "I'm not either."

A few minutes later, Eugene had a contorted walking stick. Now he had to find an Indian relic he could take home. Then each would have a stick and an archaeological find. Ron and Eric had promised to help tote the big stone home if he found nothing smaller.

Hours and minutes meant little to these three teenagers eager to explore nature. The time used to discover the twisted walking stick, the moonshine still, and the "Mortar Bowl" consumed most of the afternoon. Arriving back at camp at around six o'clock, Ron suggested he cook potatoes and open a can of pork and beans for supper. The other two readily agreed; they were all hungry. The trio chowed down with a baked potato, a generous helping of pork and beans, cucumbers, and concluded the meal with chocolate brownies, baked by Eugene's mother, Mrs. West.

After they finished eating, they agreed to explore the part of the cave where they discovered the cap. They took flashlights and entered the first large cavern and crawled through the opening to the inter-chamber. The earlier discovery of the cap was on the left part of the ledge. The next time they entered this cavern, the cap somehow mysteriously moved to the right side. As they stood, all three flashlight beams began searching for the hat. They looked to the right on the ledge; it was not there. All three light beams moved along the ledge to the left; the cap was not there.

Eric exclaimed, "Now wait one minute, what is going on?"

The light beams flashed in all directions; one on the cavern's ceiling, one on the far wall, and one on the floor. Suddenly, Ron yelled, "There it is!" His light was on the cap.

Eugene said, "Now how do you suppose it got up there?"

There, it conspicuously hung on the pillar-like vertical partition, six feet above the floor.

Eric asked, "Now, how did that cap get there? Do either of you have a suggestion?"

"Here is my thought," Ron said, "A raccoon may have pushed it to the other side of the ledge, but a raccoon could not hang a cap on that partition."

Eugene silently stood, just staring at the cap. He walked over to the partition and reached for it.

Eric said, "Wait a minute, we need to talk about how that cap got there."

Eugene backed off and said, "I have no clue."

"Ron, do you have an idea what hung it six-feet above the floor?"

"Nope."

"Eugene?"

"Nope."

"I think it was hung there by someone," Eric declared.

"Someone, who?"

"Ron, I don't know, but that is the only way it could have been hung that far above the floor. Someone is trying to tell us something."

"Now, come on Eric," Eugene said. "Who is telling us what?"

"I don't know, but I have an idea."

Eugene said, "I hope you're not going to suggest that Culhwick's ghost did it."

Ron suggested, "Let's leave the cap where it is, get out of here, go back to camp, and talk about the possibilities. It's a little eerie thinking about what or who hung that cap."

That idea was plaudit.

The back chills became suffused again, not just up the spine and across the shoulders, but over Eric's whole back. The trio was soon in camp. The sun illuminated the dark clouds in the western horizon; lightning danced throughout the elongated raincloud.

As the three sat on the bank with feet hanging just above the water, Ron said, "Okay, Eric, let's have it."

"Have what?" Eric answered smiling.

"You know what I mean."

Eugene followed with, "Yeah, what is the idea you have about how that cap got hung on the partition."

"Well, my idea is this: someone is trying to frighten us."

"Why?" Ron asked. "For what reason would anyone want to scare us?"

Eugene added, "Do you think Ron's brother, Larry, or your brother, Tom, is trying to scare us?"

"No, Tom is away working, and Larry doesn't know about the cave."

Ron was quick to ask, "Well, who do you think it could be?"

"I'm not sure who, but I think I know why."

Eugene impatiently asked, "Why?"

Eric said, "In the morning, I think we need to visit that moonshine still again."

Frowning, Ron asked, "What does the still have to do with the baseball cap?"

"Someone is using the still to make moonshine, and they realize we know where it is, so they are moving the cap to frighten us."

Eugene said, "We visited it twice, the last time we camped, and today. There was no sign of its use."

"Remember that half-hidden path on the other side of the still that we didn't notice the first time?"

Ron was quick to point out, "If you remember, the beaten path to the stream was used more than the other one."

Eric looked at a curious Ron, and said, "Hello, two paths, one above the still and one below the still, one doesn't show much use, while the other is well beaten and shows a lot of frequent use."

Eugene inserted, "Oh, so you think someone is afraid that we will reveal the whereabouts of his still?"

Rod added, "He doesn't want us around the still, right?"

Eugene followed with, "I hope he's not a violent swashbuckler."

Ron said, "Me too."

"I believe that is the most plausible thing," Eric said. He continued, "In the morning, we need to visit that still again."

"For what?" quizzed Eugene.

"Yeah, what are we looking for?"

Eric answered, "We need to look at that path on the other side of the still. I wonder how far it goes and if it shows use away from the still."

Ron asked, "Eric, what are you suggesting?"

"We didn't notice it the first time, and today we didn't look at it very close. Someone might have tried to hide it."

The boys talked long into the night about Indian relics, the cap, the moonshine still, and the uncertain dangers of their nameless trickster. Not one mentioned the new find, Eugene's twisted contorted walking stick. It lay with the others against a small pine tree behind the fire ring. Was it also just another worthless stick, or would a memorable experience give it some value? The fire blaze over the three logs was scintillating; there was a slight rustle through the bush just behind the sleeping teenagers.

CHAPTER 13

DISCOVERY OF A NEW PATH

ERIC AND RON AWOKE TO THE SMELL OF scrambled eggs, hot sage sausage, and flatbread toast heating in a skillet over a blazing campfire. As Eric got up and moved over to the campfire, Eugene handed him a full breakfast plate.

Taking it, he said, "Thanks. Where is my water?"

"See the water spurting out of that rock over there?" Eugene continued as he prepared Ron a plate, "Just jump over the creek and help yourself."

As the trio sat on the bank eating, the Friday morning sun began to shine with a soft glow over the pine trees, disseminating the tree level fog. After the fog lifted, they left the campsite and followed the disturbed route of yesterday and cautiously arrived at the still.

Eric spoke first, "I want to look at the lower path again, more closely this time."

At the end of the path, a pool of clear water bubbled out of the ground. Eric said, "The other day I noticed a three-foot wide pool, but this looks deep."

Ron said, "I'll measure it." Placing his walking stick on the bottom of the pool, he was surprised at the depth, he said, "It's at least three feet deep."

"So?" Eugene questioning asked.

Trying to make sense of the smooth beaten-down path, a large deep waterhole, and the moonshine still, Eric answered, "If someone is moonshining, and I think they are, they need fresh water."

Ron was quick to add, "Yeah, this pool is deep enough to fill a five-gallon bucket with one dip."

Eugene asked, "Why would they need water? I thought they carried the liquid from the 'sour mash' and poured it into the steel container with the copper tubing to make moonshine."

"Well, maybe they need cold water to cool down the tubing, or maybe for drinking water or maybe to prevent fires," Eric answered. "These environs are perfect for a still; it would be difficult for the authorities to find it in all of this growth of vines, briars, and new saplings."

Eugene suggested, "Don't you think we should be quiet?"

The three agreed that it would be undesirable to be noticed on the third visit to the moonshine area. They would use extreme caution around the still area.

After arriving, they carefully went farther up the hill. Two-hundred-feet above the still, they found the path as smooth and well used as the lower one; someone had deliberately tried to hide the path by throwing leaves and small limbs over it. Their earlier visits were known, but by whom?

"Okay," Eric whispered, "Now we know, they know, that we can identify the location of the moonshine still, and that shine is being made."

Ron was quick to add, "Yeah, and they know who we are."

"Don't you think we need to get out of here?" Eugene said as he was already fifteen-feet in the tangled mess of undergrowth.

Ron and Eric were close behind. As Eric moved away from the still, he thought, *here comes the back chills again.*

Between the moonshine still and camp was a mile of a thick tangled wild plant growth. The trio had not discovered or even thought about a path between the two locations. Sitting on the creekbank eating a sandwich, Eugene asked, "How do you suppose the trickster got from the still to the cave? You know how tough it was for us to go through that snarled tangle; there is no sign of a path where someone passed through that mess."

Considering the question, Eric said, "I never thought about that; did you, Ron?"

"No. Eric, what is our next move?"

"Okay, the way I see it, we have two options for this afternoon. One, we can walk downstream to locate a new path leading to the still area, or we can go into the cave and see if the cap has been moved."

Eugene thoughtfully spoke, "We don't need sunshine for the cave, but we need it to walk the creek."

Ron jumped up, declared, "Off down the creek we go!"

The trio grabbed walking sticks and wandered along the edge of the stream for five hundred yards when Eugene pointed to a small tree several feet in front of them.

Eric stopped, looked at the bush and said, "What about it?"

"See, it is all bent over. A little strange, isn't it?"

While Eric and Eugene stood discussing the odd leaning tree, Ron walked over to it. He pulled the bush upright and said, "Hey Eugene, you've found something; come look."

Sure enough, someone had partially hidden a trail. It was well-used and led uphill toward the moonshine still.

All three stood looking up the partially concealed trail.

Eric said, "Now what?"

Ron came back with, "Yeah, now what?"

"What should we not do?" Eugene reaffirmed.

Eric spoke first, "I want to see where this path goes."

Ron hastily spoke, "I want to see it too, but it could be dangerous."

Eugene added, "From what I've heard, moonshiners are grievous and touchy people."

"Okay, here is what I think we should do. One, see where this trail leads; two, put the bent tree back as we found it; third, be quiet, and fourth, disturb nothing on the trail or next to it."

"I agree with Eric. How about you, Eugene?"

"Just how dangerous would it be if we got caught on the trail?"

Ron added, "What if they discover that we know where this trail is?"

Eric said, "Let's be careful. I want to see where it goes."

"Okay, Eric, you lead, I'll bring up the back," Eugene suggested.

"Sounds good to me," Ron said.

The teenagers proceeded cautiously uphill through a tunnel-like walkway, flanked by bushes, briars, and vines overhead. About one-fourth of a mile up the hill, the trail began to turn a little to the Northwest. It curved and wove through dense thickets, around fallen logs, and stumps.

Eric stopped, turned, and whispered, "How far are we from the creek?"

Ron spoke softly, "I don't know."

"I don't know either," Eugene mouthed. He added, "We've moved so slow."

"Why do you ask?" quizzed Ron.

Eric answered, "I think this path is leading back to the moonshine still site." All three had assumed that the path away from the still would lead north to the county road.

Huddled together, Eugene said, "So this is the way into the still, not from the north."

Eric spoke slowly, "That is what I'm beginning to believe."

Ron questioned, "What should we do now?"

Eric said, "I have a suggestion, you wait here, and I'll see where it leads."

"We don't want to do that," both Eugene and Ron spoke in unison.

Eric asked, "I smell smoke, don't you?"

Ron answered, "I believe I do."

"Eugene, how about you?"

Eugene replied, "I don't smell smoke but what does smelling smoke have to do with you going up the trail by yourself?"

"If this does lead to the moonshiner's still and if someone is at the site, it will be easier and quieter for me to leave than all three of us."

"Okay, you be careful," Ron instructed.

"Don't become impatient. It will take several minutes, and I want to see if our assumption is correct," Eric softly answered.

Carrying his contorted walking stick horizontally in his hand, he crept along, listening for sounds that could come from the still. When he went around a sizeable white oak tree, he found himself standing in the upper path leading away from the moonshine still area. On the earlier inspection of the trail, they had not come all the way to the oak tree. He stopped, no sound came to his ears, but he still smelled smoke. Eric stood there thinking, *I'm close to the still; should I leave now, or should I locate the smoke's origin?* He inched down the footpath until he could see the still. Easing over to the pot, he felt the burned wood below; it was still smoking. A large bucket half full of water was sitting next to the still. He hurriedly made his way back to where he had left Ron and Eugene.

As he came upon them, he whispered, "Let's get back to camp, and I'll tell you what I've found. Be quiet and no talking."

The trio hurried back to camp, eager to hear what Eric discovered. Huddled around the stream's bank-seat, Ron spoke first, "Okay, Eric, what did you find?"

"You will not believe this."

"Come on Eric, what did you find?" Eugene asked, "and why are we whispering?"

"Someone was recently making shine, maybe even yesterday."

"Why maybe yesterday? Was someone at the still?" quizzed Ron.

"No, I didn't see anyone, but the smoke we smelled was coming from smoldering wood under the pot, and a bucket half full of water was sitting next to it. That bucket was not there before."

"What did you find about the path leading away from the moonshine still?" questioned Eugene.

Eric answered, "The pathway we just discovered is part of the same trail."

Ron was quick to add, "So the entrance to this moonshine still is just a few feet below our camp."

Eugene spoke, "And the cave."

"That's right. Whoever it is might have been very close to our camp."

Ron said, "You mean they could have been listening to our conversations?"

Eugene added, "Last night?"

"Probably not at night."

Eugene asked, "Eric, why not?"

"If they did, it was during daylight. It would be too noisy walking the creek at night."

Ron added, "Yeah, and if they used lights, we would have seen them."

Eugene asked, "What should we do now?"

The three teenagers talked during supper of baked Irish potatoes, raw carrots, radishes, sliced cucumber, and cherry tomatoes. They spoke in hushed voices, frequently looking downstream.

Ron said, "Let's go to the cave, I want to see if the hat is still hanging on the wall."

Eugene jumped up and said, "Off to the cave we go."

Walking sticks in hand, all now contorted, the trio took flashlights and walked across the creek to the cavernous central opening. There was no vigilance of the interior or exterior of the cave's order on previous excursions; it would be different this time. As they cautiously advanced into the cave, they nervously looked for stone disturbances on the floor, unusual debris of leaves, twigs, or a particular arrangement of loose rock. They stopped at the entrance to the corridor leading to the innermost room.

Eric said, "Who wants to go in first?"

"Eric, I will," Ron quickly volunteered.

Eric said, "Okay, Eugene, you follow Ron, and I'll protect our back."

Ron was halfway to the large chamber, when Eugene said, "You don't have to be so anxious," turning, he jumped into the passageway crawling toward the cap room.

Eric smiled as he followed the duo. Before Eric stood upright in the inner chamber, Ron yelled, "The cap is gone!"

The cap was not on the rock partition, the floor, or the ledge; it had vanished. "Now what?" Eugene asked with tight lips and an unusual disquieting frown that covered his whole face. Eric had never seen Eugene display such a distressed look before. It was obvious that the earlier remark "I'll protect your back," was troubling to him.

"I'm sorry Eugene, I was just teasing about protecting our back." Eric trusted his apology would quickly relieve the anxiety in Eugene's mien.

Eugene said, "I'm beginning to think we don't belong in this cave; it's kind of spooky, don't you think?"

"What are you thinking?" Ron asked. "Could you be thinking about 'weird Culhwich'?"

"No, it's just eerie with the cap moving and then disappearing."

Eric walked over to Eugene, put his arm around his shoulder, and said, "There are no spooks inside this cave system, and it is okay for us to be here. Haven't I told you about a chill that starts in my lower back, goes up my spine, and across my shoulders?"

"You have."

"When this happens, I recall the Scripture found in Isaiah 7:4. It says, 'Be careful, keep calm, and don't be afraid,' so don't be scared. You know Jesus said, 'Don't be afraid' several times."

Hearing the discussion, Ron came over and said, "Eric, what's going on?"

"I was telling Eugene of the Bible verse that Uncle Esau taught me to use. We were wondering if we should be in this cave, because of the missing cap, and the moonshine still."

Ron asked, "Eric do you think Isaiah was talking about not being afraid in caves?"

"Of course not, but God does not want us to be afraid. He wants us to trust in Him and be anxious for nothing."

Adding no further comment to the discussion, Ron said, "Let's go back to the entrance and look in the other chamber."

The trio scrambled back along the crawlway, Eugene first, Ron second, and then Eric.

As the three teenagers moved along the corridor, around the slight bend, and down the gradual incline toward the sound of dripping water, they continued to hunt for the elusive cap. Examination of the inner chamber was intense. Finding nothing, they went back to the entrance to examine the tight corridor leading off to the right. Because of the constricted opening, they had not fully explored it. Eric led with the others close behind. The narrow way eventually widened until all three stood side-by-side, flashlights flashing all around. Ron pulled a book of matches out of his pocket and after striking one, he held it above his head.

Eric said, "What are you doing? We have flashlights."

When the match extinguished itself, Ron lit three more matches and raised them high before answering, "Watch that flame."

Eugene was quick to notice, "I believe it is waving a little. Do you think there is another entry in this part of the cave?"

"I don't know, but the air is certainly moving the flame down this corridor, it might be just a small opening."

Going a little farther into this section, they found an eight-inch ceiling shaft venting the air move-ment. This chamber was smaller than the other two, and after a careful search, the trio had had enough spelunking, so they returned to camp. Tonight was going to be a most anxious night for the teenagers. Countless queries roused apprehensive opinions and an unsettled frame of mind for a worried sleep-less night. Speaking with muted voices well into the morning hours, they often stopped and looked downstream listening for any strange sound. The new noises they heard tonight were: a slight breeze, rustling leaves, a bubbly sound of water flowing over a stone, raccoons moving through the undergrowth, or an occasional hoot from an owl. The sun was high in the sky when the trio awoke. Eating all the remaining food, they departed for home, promising to camp again.

CHAPTER 14

REVISIT THE CAVE & MOONSHINE STILL

(1956–1957) THE LATE SPRING SEASON progressed into summer, then into harvest time for the Bray, Milford, and West families. The teenagers did not have another chance to explore the moonshine still or the cave. The disappearance of the cap was still a mystery; the questionable knowledge of how much the still owner knew, was troubling. School was to begin next week, and the freshman trio was eager to attend the Algebra class taught by Mr. Bob. They welcomed a change from eighth-grade math; it would be different from every other subject.

The first day of school came on Tuesday morning after Labor Day. Junior Brooks, a twelve-year veteran driver, gave everyone a hearty "come aboard" as he drove the old yellow student transport along the same route, picking up the children. The county school system had modernized the bus; the right front cracked tire was replaced with a retread and the left rear outside tire with a half-worn tire. The left mirror was replaced, but the broken loose-fitting windows still rattled along the rough gravel road. The state replaced the rickety steel bridge across Buck Creek with a new modern concrete structure; no more unloading the bus and walking across the dangerous bridge. As usual, the three sat on the front seat, just behind the driver.

Ron asked, "Eric, I'm looking forward to Algebra, aren't you?"

"Yes, I am."

"Me too," Eugene added. "Neither Mom nor Dad know much about it."

"Ron, your brother Larry is good in math; did he explain it to you?" quizzed Eric.

"Yes, he likes math, and he explained it this way: Algebra uses symbols to represent quantities without fixed values."

"I thought a quantity was a number, like four, ten, or one hundred."

"Eugene, the way Larry explained it, a quantity can be represented by anything if everyone agrees to the same thing."

Eric said, "You're saying that an 'X' could mean five, nine, fifty, or even a thousand if everyone agreed, right?"

"I think so; Larry says that is the reason they are called variables."

Junior broke into the conversation when he asked, "You fellows been camping lately?"

Eric answered, "Yeah, we camped for three days in early June."

"Did you find what repositioned the cap?" he asked. He was inquiring about the cap being shuffled from the left side to the far right on the shelf.

Eric leaned over the rail behind Junior and whispered, "Junior, the cap was moved from left to the right side, then it was hung on a partition six-feet above the floor. We haven't told anyone yet."

Continuing to speak softly, he said, "Really, I'll have to go camping with you boys sometime."

When the word "really" was spoken by Junior, it had an unusual suggestive knowledge of the camping trips; but this insinuation remained elusive to the trio.

After a few days in Algebra, the teenagers adapted to the radical change in math, and the encouragement and patience of Mr. Bob overshadowed the difficulty of the unknowns. The three were together in Math, English, Social Studies, Agriculture, Physical Education, and study hall. One day in Physical Education class, just before Christmas break, Mr. Shelby, the teacher, grouped the all-boys class for tumbling exercises. Each student had to run toward a rolled-up tumbling mat, place both hands on the foot-high roll, then flip onto another flat mat, landing on their feet. Ron dashed toward the mat, put his hands on the roll, and flipped beautifully and landed standing on the flat mat. Eugene followed with the same result; he turned smiling, lifted both hands illustrating the simplicity of this assignment. Eric was next in line. However, he stepped aside to let Alford go. Eric remained out of line to allow the next in line, Albert, to go. Then Mr. Shelby said, "Bray, what's wrong? You're next, now let's go."

A little embarrassed, Eric ran toward the roll, and at just the right time he leaped toward the roll putting both hands on it. His momentum was not enough to propel his feet on over to the flat mat, so he became stationary with hands on the rolled-up tumbling mat and his feet pointing toward the gym's roof. He had never looked at the gym ceiling from this angle before. Losing his hold, his vertical 180-pound body came crashing down, head first, on the hard mat, then falling sideways to the hard maple gym floor. By the time Eric rolled over on his back, Mr. Shelby had rushed over and said, "Eric, don't move yet. How is your neck? Are you hurt?"

Sitting up, Eric answered, "I don't think so. My neck popped though."

"You need to lie down on the bleacher the rest of the period; your neck will probably be a little sore in the morning."

In January, after Christmas break, the trio settled into the second-semester classes. There was another physical education incident that the teenagers discussed. Mr. Shelby conditioned the freshman class with seven months of running, pushups, jumping jacks, arm twirls, and sit-ups. One day he announced that he would give a preview of the only determining factor to receive an "A" for the second semester. If a student attended all classes and participated, he would receive a B; missing three classes without an excuse, a C; missing five to seven, a D; and missing eight or more, an F. All except one thin, pallid youngster were farm teenagers; Albert recently moved from Indiana. To receive an A, the students laid on the floor, shoulder to shoulder, and Mr. Shelby moved from student to student standing on each boy's stomach; he weighed 120 pounds. As he moved from Eric's left and stood towering above, he stopped, looked down, and said, "Enjoyable day, isn't it, Mr. Bray?"

Through clenched teeth, Eric answered, "Yes sir."

Stepping from Eric to Ron, he looked down at him and said, "Pleasant day, isn't it, Mr. Milford?"

As he placed his feet on Eugene's stomach, Eugene smiled and said, "Pleasing day, teach."

When Mr. Shelby reached the end of students lying on the floor, he cautiously placed only one foot on the slender boy's midsection and asked, "Albert, want me to stand on your stomach?"

"Mr. Shelby, please, just give me a B. Maybe next year I'll be as strong as the rest of my classmates."

The amicable trio received an A for the semester.

Graduation occurred in late May with some of the graduating seniors having the aspiration of college attendance in the fall. The class of thirty-six, five had the ambition of becoming elementary teachers, two wanted to study for a law degree, three enrolled in vocational/technical school immediately after graduation, two wanted to become nurses, and one quiet, reserved boy planned to enter medical school.

Larry, Ron's brother, entered vocational/technical school; Tom, Eric's brother, had landed a high-paying government job; Julie was now a senior, and Eric; Ron, and Eugene would be sophomores in the fall. On the way home, the trio planned another camping trip.

Eugene asked, "Eric, when can we camp?"

Eric, now a sophomore, replied, "I have to help dad installed a septic system for the inside bathroom, so we can have a shower, maybe we can go then." Now the Brays household was modernized with a shower, a refrigerator, an electric water heater, and a cook stove.

Eric had other chores to do such as: milking, feeding chickens, feeding pigs, gardening, picking strawberries, setting tobacco, and making molasses.

Ron spoke up and said, "I can go anytime."

Eugene added, "Me too."

Eric said "Okay, after we finish the septic system, cultivating and spraying the tobacco for worms, and picking strawberries, I can go; maybe in late June."

Three weeks later, early Thursday morning, after completing the chores, Eric met Ron and Eugene at the bridge. Being sophomores and somewhat experienced spelunkers, all three teenagers came with full backpacks, contorted walking sticks, and an eagerness to locate the cap, and visit the moonshine still again. This time, all three would be highly alert inside the cave, and on another close scrutinized expedition to the still. They were amazed as they passed by the beautiful thirty-foot waterfall with its airborne mist floating upward and disappearing in midair. They sat on the creek bank for a few minutes before moving on downstream; all three still amazed by the peaceful tranquil and unspoiled majestic charm.

Arriving at the clearing, Eugene suggested, "Let's arrange camp a little different than before; let's move the sleeping area deeper into the pine thicket. We can still use the same fire ring for cooking."

Ron asked, "Why do you want to move deeper into the trees?"

Without answering, Eugene threw his pack to the ground and removed two stacks of empty metal cans. To save space in his backpack, he had inserted small ones into the larger ones.

Watching Eugene separate the cans, Eric asked, "What are you doing with all those empty cans?"

"If we move our sleeping bags back into the thicket, I want to tie these cans to a string on the perimeter to alert us if anyone snoops around."

Ron said, "That is a clever idea." He added, "I could have brought three small goat bells that would have rattled with the slightest movement."

"Boy, what a salient suggestion. Do I perceive someone is frightened?"

"Now Eric, you know that there is clandestine behavior by someone and we should be prepared; Dad taught me always to be careful."

"Oh, I agree, that's a good idea. I was joshing you; let's do it."

The trio immediately acted on Eugene's proposal. Small pine trees were cleared with the all-steel hatchet to make adjacent spaces for the sleeping bags; then a continuous string was strung twenty-feet deep into the trees around the perimeter. The cans were hung in clusters of three around the shelter. A joint decision had to be made on the investigative plan. What were they going to do about the missing cap and the moonshine still? What did they want to accomplish on this camping trip?

Eric said, "Okay, let's list the things we want to do and then we'll carry them out."

163

Ron was quick to jump in, "I want to know how that cap moved and who made it disappear."

"Yes," Eugene added, "I want to know if that path downstream is the only one leading to the still."

Eric spoke with a disturbed look, "I want to look farther downstream to see if someone might be coming in and out from the south because when we first discovered the moonshine still, I thought I knew who it was—someone living just north of it."

Ron suggested, "How about this: let's look in the cave first and then search downstream, then in the morning we can go to the still?"

"Good idea. How about you, Eric?"

"I'm okay with that."

Ron proposed, "We're familiar with the cave's layout, so let's go and find that cap."

The trio entered the large frontal opening of the cave and progressed to the crawl-through carrying only flashlights and walking sticks. No return string was necessary because of the numerous times they had visited this part. Crawling through the corridor, they stood upright in the first inner-chamber, the shelf was along one wall and the partition on the other side. Finding the cap on the left side of the ledge, they hurriedly left and when they returned it was found on the far right of the shelf. The third visit to this chamber, the cap was hanging six-feet above the floor on the top of the partition, and on the last visit, it had disappeared. Now it was time for these sophomores to find the cap or its connection to the moonshine still. Was Eric's assumption correct: that someone wanted to scare them and keep the moon-shining business a secret? A thorough inspection revealed no cap; nothing else had been disturbed. The triad returned to the frontal opening and shuf-fled down the left corridor to the cavern of running water, stalactites, and stalagmites. An extended search around the stalagmites offered no additional information, so an intense study of the jagged sta-lactites began.

"Eugene, you go around to the far side and Ron, you go around this side, and I'll stay in the middle," instructed Eric.

Ron asked, "Why?"

"There is an odd shadow about eight feet off the floor; it might be a flat place."

Taking their position, three flashlights illuminated all sides of the hanging ceiling rock. There appeared to be an opening through the poorly formed stalactites.

"Eugene come over here. You are the lightest; Ron and I will hold you up, so you can see the top."

As they pushed him above the top rim, he excitedly yelled, "Give me my stick."

Ron asked, "What's wrong?"

Eric added, "What's wrong, Eugene?"

"That cap is up here, and I don't want to touch it, I want to look at it."

It was just an ordinary ballcap, no legs, no wings, no ears, and no eyes, but how did it get transferred to various spots inside the cave?

Eric spoke first, "Let's return the cap, go back to camp, eat lunch, and then go to the moonshine still."

"I agree," Eugene said. "I have another proposition."

Eric looked at Ron and said, "Ron, I thought we knew him."

Ron was quick to follow, "What's the proposition?"

Eugene reached into his pocket and pulled out a half-used spool of general-purpose gray thread.

"Now, what do you want to do with that thread? Tie someone up?"

"Eric, as we leave, let's tape this gray thread across the entrance to this chamber, tape one low and one high. An animal will break only the low one, and a person will probably break both."

Ron said, "That's an ingenious idea, but where's the tape?"

Eugene had already pulled a small roll from his hip pocket and said smiling, "Will this do?"

"I'm impressed, Eugene," Eric said, "Let's do it."

"This way we can determine if someone is sneaking in after dark or when we are away."

"Eugene are you saying that maybe raccoons are moving this cap?" Ron doubtfully asked.

Eugene answered, "They play with everything, and if two or three started to play and chased each other, yes, I think they could be responsible for the cap movement on the ledge; not probably, but yes, possibly. They couldn't have hung it on the partition."

Eric added, "I agree."

They returned to camp after stringing the thread across the narrow corridor leading to the stalactite room. The thread would blend with the rock wall and be difficult to see, even with a flashlight. Eating a lunch of cucumbers, radishes, and peanut butter and jam sandwiches, they drank from the crystal-clear water that spouted from the rock wall across the branch; they are now prepared for the second part of the plan. Taking their contorted walking sticks, hatchet, and hunting knives, they commenced combing the banks below the trail that was partially concealed by a bush. One hundred feet downstream, the bank became solid limestone rock touching the water's edge and then it ended twelve feet away from the stream in thick knee-high bushes. From this rock outbreak, the banks downstream became high and overgrown with vines and shrubs growing in crevices of the sheer-rock wall. Returning to the limestone outcrop, they sat down to discuss their failure in locating a southern access to the path. Sitting with knees drawn up and arms placed on them, they began to analyze their lack of finding evidence that supported their premise.

Eric spoke first, "I still believe that someone comes up this creek and uses that moonshine still."

"We've been careful to watch and examine every part of the bank on both sides of the branch. I don't think we've missed anything, do you, Ron?"

"We haven't missed a thing, no footprints, no disturbance, nothing unusual on either side. The creek's bottom below here is tough to walk in; it has ledges, round rock, and deep places."

After several minutes, Eric got to his feet and said, "What's on the other side of this big rock?"

"It disappears under those bushes and then dense growth," Eugene pointed out.

Climbing the rock's slight incline to the scrubs, Eric turned and said, "You fellows come and see what is on the other side of these bushes."

Ron and Eugene climbed the rock and hurried to see where Eric was pointing, apparently a well-used path; the growth hid the entrance from the branch.

"So, I was not wrong; things are beginning to take shape."

Frowning, Eugene asked, "Taking shape. Are you saying that what you first thought is now making sense?"

"Well, now we know for sure someone is making moonshine and that someone is coming from the south, not the north, and it is not the person I thought it was. Furthermore, I don't have the slightest idea who is moonshining."

Ron chipped in with, "Eric, I don't see an elucidation of the cap's movement, who, or why, I believe your shape is crystal clear, see-through, transparent. . ."

"You know what I mean. Let's go back to camp."

The trio decided to inspect the gray thread stratagem before going back to camp. Entering the frontal chamber, they found the thread still hung across the left corridor walkway.

Eugene suggested, "Why don't we string that small round opening leading to the first cavern?"

After taping string across the two-foot opening of the entrance to the twelve-foot-long passageway to the number one chamber, they returned to camp. Laying on their bedrolls, the triad talked extensively about the possibilities of the cave and moonshine still. The conversation began to wane when Eric, being good at initiating biblical stories, said, "I'm reminded of a story in the Bible about a string; do either of you remember it?"

Ron looked at Eugene who was shaking his head and said, "Why don't you tell us about it?"

"You remember the Samson story in Judges 16:12, don't you?"

They both said in unison, "Yes."

Eric continued, "Well, Delilah tied Samson with new ropes so that the Philistines could subdue him, and he broke the ropes off his arms like a thread."

Ron was quick to respond, "Yeah, I recall the story now. Samson led Israel as a judge for twenty years. . ."

"And he had supernatural power," Eugene added.

"That's right. Samson had taken a Nazirite vow, set apart to God from birth, Judges 13:5, and he was never to shave his head."

"He told Delilah this secret, and she told his enemies, then the Philistines cut his hair, and he lost his strength."

The sleeping trio chatted past midnight and was abruptly awakened Friday morning before daylight by the clanging of hanging metal cans and the clanking of dishes that reverberated up and down the creek. Throwing off the sleeping bags and jumping to their feet, all three immediately retrieved their trusty contorted walking sticks. Their quick movement instantly put them in a defense stance armed with only sticks against what could be a lurking wildcat, a prowling panther, a two-thousand-pound raging bull, or an angry moonshiner loaded for the Feds, with a double-barreled shotgun. When three

171

heartbeats gradually returned to near normal, Eric said, "See anything?"

"No."

Still standing in a bent stance with both hands on his stick ready to defend himself, Eric turned and in the dim firelight, observed Eugene's frightened appearance; he, too, stood in the same manner. "Eugene, you okay?"

"Yeah, I'm okay. What made all that noise?"

Holding up his hand, Ron said, "Listen."

After a few moments, Eric asked in a faint whisper, "Listen for what?"

"I thought I heard something or someone in the water."

Eugene, looking at Ron in semidarkness, quietly asked, "What kind of a sound? A gurgle, a splash, or a continuous noise, like maybe someone running?"

"I'm not sure, but I heard noise coming from downstream."

Eugene, still was not sure what woke him, said, "I think I heard something more than just the sound of water."

"That was all those empty cans you tied around the camp."

"Oh, I'm sorry Ron. I had already forgotten about my alarm system, but I thought I heard the clatter of dishes and pans."

"You did," explained Eric. "I think the raccoon family turned our dishes over, got scared, and ran through Eugene's alarm system."

Eugene asked, "What about the noise Ron heard coming from downstream?"

"Ron was it loud or just a splash?"

"Probably a splash," he answered.

"I think a group of raccoons got frightened and ran every which way," Eric concluded. He added, "They've been visiting us every night, hoping to get a little food."

Ron added, "You're probably right."

"I agree," Eugene said. "Sounds logical to me."

The trio sat down on their sleeping bags still a little jittery. Eugene asked, "Eric, what time is it?"

Looking at the moon hanging low in the western sky, he said, "It's well past midnight; the moon was in the east when we went to bed. It's probably about four-thirty or five."

Ron asked, "Who woke up first?"

Eugene explained, "When I first realized I was awake, you were standing to my left holding your stick, and Eric was to my right holding his, and I think I was holding mine."

Ron said, "Eugene, I'm surprised that one of us didn't grab the hatchet."

"Me too," Eric added. "Were either of you scared?"

"I don't know if I was scared," Eugene said, "but it was certainly a little unnerving."

Ron added, "My heart sure was beating fast."

"I think we were all startled with shaky knees, kind of like King Belshazzar," laughed Eric.

Eugene asked, "Is that another Bible story?"

Ron, wanting to be part of the conversation, said, "That was when he saw something written on a wall, wasn't it?"

Eric retrieved the Bible from his backpack and turned to Daniel chapter five. He read the first five verses before saying, "Listen to this. Verse six, 'His face turned pale, and he was so frightened that his knees knocked together, and his legs gave way.'"

Eugene said, "I don't know if my face was pale, but I was sure frightened."

"Me too," Ron laughingly added, "and my knees were knocking too."

Then Eric said with a smile, "I think we were all startled instead of scared or frightened, right?"

Eugene agreed. He said, "That sounds better."

"That's a good idea, Eric, especially when we retell this experience."

The teenagers enjoyed recalling the incident, but all agreed that no knees gave way.

The conversation of suddenly awaking, unusual frightening sounds, the possibility of the trickster invading their camp, and body chills continued until morning. Now the three had a shared experience with this worthless stick; ever so small of an occurrence at the time, the willingness to protect the other would be remembered for a lifetime. The future reminiscing about this intense teenager incident would always start like, "Remember the time we went camping and were scared by a bunch of raccoons?"

After an early Friday morning breakfast, the inspection of Eugene's stratagem plan was paramount. Upon entering the frontal chamber, they moved to the long twelve-foot passageway; the gray thread was still detectable across the opening. The teenagers refocused attention to the entry of the left passageway.

When Ron was about to grab the string, Eugene said, "Wait, don't do that."

Puzzled at Eugene's hasty caution, Eric said, "Eugene, since this was your plan, why don't you examine the tape and the thread, then tell us what happened."

The top tape on the right wall was hanging down; it was connected only by one end. So was the bottom tape that was ten-inches above the floor. He then inspected the other side; both ends of the top tape were still fastened to the wall and the thread hanging from it. Lifting the thread with a toothpick, he let it slide along to the end. The bottom tape was the same; both ends of the tape were attached to the wall with the thread still attached to it. Eugene took another toothpick from his shirt pocket and let the bottom thread slide along to the end.

Standing for several minutes watching Eugene go through this exercise, Eric and Ron became more mystified than by his sudden "Don't do that." Both wanted to ask but hesitated. Finally, Eugene stood and announced his findings.

"Someone has been here."

Surprised at his proclamation, Ron said, "How did you determine that someone caused the strings to fall?"

"Yeah," Eric added, "Maybe a raccoon caused the bottom thread to come loose, and the dampness affected the other one."

Ignoring the pessimistic remarks, Eugene pointing to the bottom tape and string said, "I put some sticky tree resin on the string to catch hair if a raccoon went under it; there was no hair on the thread. The thread was pulled entirely out of the tape on the one side; so, something big, like a person, had to walk through this passageway to do that."

Grinning Eric said, "Could Culhwich's ghost do it?"

Eugene grinned and said, "Eric, you are funny; he's droll, isn't he, Ron?"

"Mirthful, I would say, mirthful," he replied with a smile.

Eugene endured the good-natured lighthearted teasing; it was time to venture further down this left corridor to the stalagmites and stalactites to determine if the cap was still there. The same procedure was used to lift Eugene high enough to investigate the small cache above the stalactites. As his eye crested the outer rim, he yelled, "The cap is gone!"

The trio stood looking at each other with perplexed expressions on their faces. "Let's search this cave for that cap!"

They combed every nook and corner of the chamber for the cap or other evidence of the would-be trickster; for thirty minutes every rock was intensely scrutinized, then the teenagers moved to the chamber passageway leading off to the right of the frontal cavern. They searched and examined the entire cave system for hours and found absolutely nothing, no cap nor any trace of it, only threads hanging by one end. Perplexed, the would-be detectives silently returned to camp. It was lunchtime, but many unanswered questions dulled the hunger pangs of these adventurous teenagers.

Eugene unmistakably showed frustration when he said, "I want to see that moonshine still again!"

Ron followed, "Me too!"

"Let's eat lunch," Eric said, "then we will go."

After lunch, the trio walked downstream to the concealed path hidden by the bent bush, then continued uphill toward the still. They came to the large oak tree, walked boldly around the corner straight toward the still. Aghast at what they saw, they became motionless, mouths open, speechless, dumbfounded, and disquieted. Several moments passed before they were able to speak at this astonishing scene; sitting conspicuously on the very top of the moonshine still, sat the cap. Seconds before speech returned to any of the three, a thunderous breaking of a limb echoed just beyond the oak tree. Without saying a word, Eric turned and dashed toward the sound; the others followed close behind. Rounding the bend at the same time, they leaped over small bushes along the beaten down path. There the arm-size limb laid; alongside a grown man laid face down. The teenage trio tackled the prone figure; as they struggled to restrain him, he began to chuckle. Ron looked at Eric and Eugene, shrugged his shoulders and said, "Turn him over."

Turning the man over, he giggled and laughed; then it turned into a hysterical emotional outburst. The boys fell backward to a sitting position staring at the figure laying on his back in front of them. It was the bus driver, Junior Brooks. The boys began to laugh; Junior laughed so long and hard he started holding his sides with tears flowing down both cheeks. The exuberant laughter continued for five minutes before Eric spoke, "Junior, what in the world are you doing here?"

Ron asked, "Did you put that hat on the still?"

Before he could answer, Eugene asked, "Have you been moving that cap in the cave?"

Junior had another laughter outburst; he tried to talk between surges of laughing, wiping tears off his cheeks, and holding his sides. After he calmed down, with the broadest smile the boys had ever seen him have, he said, "I sure had you boys going, didn't I?"

Eugene insisted he answer his question, "Did you move the cap in the cave?"

"I moved it from the ledge to the partition."

"Did you move it from the partition to the stalactite room?"

"Yes."

Eric chipped in, "I guess you brought it here and put in on the moonshine still?"

Still laughing, Junior said, "Yes."

Eugene had forgotten one cap move and asked, "Junior did you move the cap from the left side of the ledge to the right side?"

"No, I did not."

"Well, how did it get moved?"

"I don't know; maybe a raccoon moved it. I think they stay in that part in freezing weather."

Ron sitting there befuddled amid the questioning, answering and laughter, and finally said, "How did you get to the cave without us seeing or hearing you?"

Sitting up, Junior pointed to the bushes next to him and said, "There are open woods just over these bushes, so I parked my car on the road, came through the woods, over the bushes, down the path, and up the branch and right into the cave. It would take a bad thunderstorm to wake you."

After all the laughter had subsided, the foursome moved down the beaten path to the campsite.

With a puzzled look on his face, Ron said, "I still have a question or two."

"Fire away," came from a smiling Junior.

"How did you know about the moonshine still? We made a pact and told no one."

"You boys sat directly behind me on the bus, and I heard you whisper about it, and I had a general idea of the location."

"Okay, what about the smoldering fire under the still that Eric discovered?"

"I squirted lighter fluid on it and set it afire; I heard you say you wanted to see the still again."

Eric sat there listening to the questions and answers, said, "Junior, you should have stayed with us."

"I thought about it, but I was having too much fun moving the cap. I stayed hidden in the pine trees at night for a while to hear you talk. Eugene, remember your alarm system clanging a long time this morning? That was me. I tied a string on your system and rattled it from seventy feet away, so I could leave without you seeing me."

"Junior, another question: what caused you to break that large limb when we tackled you?"

"Eric, I was hiding in the bushes on the other side of the tree. I thought one of you saw me, so I ran and jumped over the wrong bush, right onto that rotten limb."

Junior agreed to spend the night with them. During supper and well into the night, conversation centered around the inquisitive compulsion of the three, what shifted the cap from left to right on the cave's ledge, who was using the moonshine still, when it was used, and one unresolved question was how the path stayed beaten down if no one was using it daily. Plans to return to solve these mysteries would include the bus driver, Junior Brooks.

CHAPTER 15

FOURSOME CAMPING TRIP- SOPHOMORE YEAR

(1957–1958) AS THE DOORS OPENED ON the updated yellow student transport, Junior Brooks, the driver, greeted each student to "come aboard." One of the three broken loose-fitted windows had been changed, both front tires replaced with retreads, the engine had been tuned, and a new tire was placed on the outside rear dual wheel. The three teenagers claimed the seat directly behind the driver. They would include Junior in their future adventurous activities; sometimes as an advisor, and other times as a comrade. The trio scheduled all classes and study hall together; they even walked across campus to the lunch room building that sat conspicuously by itself on Eubank's main street and ate together. After eating, sometimes they walked across the street to the Industrial Arts building to help the teacher, Mr. Worley, clean and put away tools. He was establishing a new educational program for the seventh through the twelfth grade. When they were unable to help Mr. Worley, the trio returned to the library to search for new books to take home or read a magazine or the newspaper. Sometimes, the librarian, Miss Samantha, ate lunch a few minutes later than the threesome, so the double-doors of the library were locked. On Monday, Eric wanted to enter the library to read the local newspaper. He asked Eugene to pick the locking-bolt to open one of the doors.

"I can't do that," he said.

"I just want to read the newspaper; I won't bother anything."

Turning to Ron, Eric said, "Can you open it?"

"I could, but I don't want to get in trouble. Why don't you open it?"

"Maybe I will," Eric responded.

Eugene said, "I'm going to the restroom."

"Me too," Ron said as he followed Eugene.

With his buddies gone, Eric looked around; no one was in the hall. Retrieving his three-bladed knife from his pocket, he opened the middle blade, placed it on the bolt and moved it backward. With a little backward pressure on the door to keep the bolt from slipping back in the locked position, Eric moved the point to a new location on the bolt, then he released the slight pressure and pushed the bolt backward again, away from the strike plate. The door stood slightly ajar. Hearing someone coming down the hallway, Eric stepped away from the door, pretending to be going to the restroom. When Albert walked around the corner, he asked, "Is the library open?"

Eric answered, "I haven't been in. Why don't you check the door?"

Albert walked to the door, grasped the knob, pulled and said, "It's open. Let's go in. I want to read a magazine."

Eric said, "Okay," and followed him in.

Albert looked at the magazine, and then he left as other students entered. Just behind them came the meticulous librarian, Miss Samantha, who was not only finicky in the arrangement of books, magazines, and newspapers, but also in controlling entry and use of the materials stored therein.

Standing on the top step with the right elbow cradled in her left hand, the right hand supporting the chin, she scanned suspiciously the occupants. Then she demanded, "Who opened this door?"

"Albert came in front of me, the door was unlocked," Eric said.

She asked, "Where is Albert?"

Wilma, a senior, answered, "He just left."

Two other students stated that the door was standing ajar when they entered.

Again, on Wednesday, Miss Samantha found the door open. Standing on the top step postured the same way as Monday, she demanded, "Who opened this door?" Today, she exhibited a slight smile while waiting for a response; she was well known for her discernment in the handling of naughty students.

Ron and Eugene had returned from the restroom and sat at Eric's table; both glanced in Eric's direction with an inquisitive expression. A quick look at Eric with their eyebrows raised suggested, "Well, answer the question!"

Eric, while looking at the newspaper, said, "Jack was in here when I came in."

Eugene leaned over and whispered, "Be sure your sin will find you out" Numbers 32:23, (KJV).

"Jack, did you unlock the door?"

"No, Miss Samantha, it was already unlocked," he nervously answered.

She stood there scanning the occupants. Unknown to Eric, she recalled those who were present at the previous mysterious unlocked doors; later in his life, Eric realized she probably knew at that time who the perpetrator was.

The following Monday as Eric leaned over the door with his pocket knife ready to move the bolt, he suddenly felt a flurry of whacks across his shoulders. It startled him so much, he jumped against the doors, dropped his knife, and turned to see Miss Samantha scowling at him. Frowning, she said, "Young man, what am I going to do with you?"

Eugene walked around the corner and saw the deadbolt trickster exposed. As he passed by to enter the library, he said, "I told you so."

Eric suddenly remembered the Scripture Eugene had referenced almost a week ago: "Be sure your sin will find you out." Something spoke to Eric's soul: *why am I lying?* Then Eric reasoned, *I really didn't lie. she never asked me directly if I opened the door. I just unlocked it.* This inconsistent thought did not match his Christian training; his soul was troubled.

Miss Samantha had hidden in the Social Studies room opposite the double-doors to catch the perpetrator.

She had not eaten, so his punishment was to bring her a lunch tray. Understanding that other students wanted and needed to do research, this arrangement continued for the spring semester. She understood impish boys and allowed Eric to check out as many as ten books over Christmas break.

Contemplating the Scripture that Eugene referenced, Eric became more troubled. Even though he had brought Miss Samantha lunch, his distressed spirit was not relieved.

Eric had been ridiculed the entire school year by a new boy, Mike Coffey, from Michigan. He had mocked his pronunciation of many words, never in the classroom with the instructor present, but in the hallways and during lunch. Ron and Eugene suggested all three confront him and if necessary, challenge him to a fight. Eric's father had taught him never to start a fight, but he could defend himself; so, the answer he gave them was "no." One day, the trio came from the lunchroom and headed to the gym for the next class. Mike was leaning against the high school building, and as Eric passed, Mike tried to trip him. When Eric saw Mike's right foot come out for the trip, Eric was just beginning his step. With a quick, hard, and forcible swing, Eric's hard steel-toed work boot struck Mike's foot just below the ankle, turning him around. Mike had to catch the building to keep from falling. The three teenagers continued around the corner to the gym, assuming Mike would follow to engage in a confrontation, but apparently, he couldn't walk on that foot. Entering the gym, Ron turned to Eric and stated, "Is that the way we are to treat our enemies?" Matthew 5:44, (KJV)

Eugene said, "Do you recall our Sunday school lesson three weeks ago about Jesus trying to counter the Jewish teachings that they should hate people who were not Jewish?"

"Yeah." Eric added, "Jesus encourages us to think the best of all people."

"People, even from Michigan?"

"Yes Ron, those from Michigan, but he never said to surrender to them," Eric reluctantly answered. "I just want him to stop bullying and mocking me."

No more bullying or mocking from Mike. The next morning, he had a slight limp.

Ron said, "We have a few minutes before class. Let's shoot some basketball."

"No, you and Eugene can, I think I'll sit here for a while," Eric answered.

A regretful feeling began to creep into Eric's consciousness as he sat on the lower bleacher. Questions began to cloud his thinking: *did I do something wrong? Will Mike dislike me even more? Will Ron and Eugene distrust or question my Christianity?* Sadness engulfed his emotions; with elbows on his knees, he bowed his head and said, "Help me Lord, if I did wrong, please forgive me and if I've harmed Ron's or Eugene's opinion of me being a Christian, please Lord, guide me in correcting that too. Lord, I also need to ask forgiveness for picking the lock on the library door."

In his youthful walk with the Lord, Eric was not aware that it was the Holy Spirit speaking to him.

A hand placed on his shoulder without warning startled him. Ron, towering above him, announced, "Class time, buddy."

The unhappy, sadness, and guilt feeling vanished.

When Eric's sophomore year ended, his sister, Julie, graduated and she anticipated studying accounting in the fall at the community college. Eric, Ron, and Eugene would be juniors in the fall. As they rode the bus home on the last day of school, they made plans for a camping trip which would include the bus driver, Junior Brooks.

Early one Thursday morning in late June of 1958, Eric led the other three along the twisty Barny Branch curves and thriving thickets with a short stop at the waterfall. The short drought diminished the water flow, but the multicolored flowering vegetation was marvelous. Junior, catching a whiff of the honeysuckle fragrance said, "Boy, what's that smell?"

Ron answered, "That's coming from the honeysuckle around the waterfall."

"I didn't know there was a waterfall near here."

"Junior," Eric said, "as you get closer to Buck Creek, this waterway runs along bluffs, overhangs, and crags, some have water, while others don't."

They moseyed downstream to the plateau surrounded by pine trees. They sat on the creek bank near the fire ring, developing plans for the day. Eric asked, "Junior, what do you think we should do?"

"Well, I've been thinking about what you boys might be getting involved with, so, I think we need to be extra careful. Didn't you tell me you found a hidden path behind the big limestone rock?"

"Yes, we were lucky to find it; it was behind the bushes."

"First, I think we should look at the moonshine still, then follow that trail south as far as it goes."

The group of four walked along the path to the oak tree, around the tree, and down to the still. The charred wood beneath the container indicated recent use. There was a pile of extra wood next to the still that had not been there on the previous visit. The bucket sitting next to it was empty. Returning to the waterway, they meandered along the tree-lined stream to the limestone outcropping. Junior led the way over the shrubs to follow the twists and turns for one-half mile before coming to a small meadow that had a lot of automobile tire tracks. Examining the tracks, Eric softly spoke, "Listen, I hear a motor."

As the vehicle approached the open field, its motor hummed and moaned, grinding its way up the hill through the rocky scrubland. Junior was quick to say, "Follow me. Let's get out of here."

The teenagers led by a middle-aged bus driver dashed back up the path to the outcrop before they stopped.

After getting his breath, Eugene asked, "Why did you want us to run?"

Eric chipped in and said, "Maybe we would have known them."

Junior replied as he searched the surroundings, "Look for a good place to hide close to the path."

"Why?"

"Ron, I want to see who, how many, and why they are coming to this remote area."

Selecting a secluded spot next to the pathway and well hidden by a blackberry thicket, the foursome lay in wait for the vehicle occupant or occupants to walk by. As they lay concealed, voices became closer and louder; there was more than one person. A muffled voice said, "Arthur, where did Ellen say we could find the shine?"

"Ellen said, your bottle is on the left, twenty-five feet from the bent tree; my bottle is forty-five on the right," Allen continued, "Why didn't George come?"

"His wife made him take her to town."

As the duo crossed over the bushes, down the outcrop, and across the creek, Junior whispered, "Everyone be quiet until they come back by."

Several minutes had passed when they heard someone splash through the water, then climb the limestone rock; one of them tripped as he strad-dled the shrubs. His obscene language describing the bush triggered a muted snicker. Arthur and Allen stumbled by the group, each clasping a quart jar; some clear liquid was already missing. Junior and the teenagers laid there until the faint sound of a motor reached them, they then moved to the campsite.

Eric thoughtfully said, "Now everything makes sense."

"Explain."

Eugene asserted, "Ron, let me guess. Eric now realizes why the path was so trodden."

Eric then continued Eugene's assertion, and said, "From Arthur's and Allen's conversation, we know that George is usually with them and that Ellen is the moonshiner or helping with the moonshine operation; that makes at least four or more using the path daily. If not daily, often."

Junior spoke, "Don't you fellows always camp on Thursday and Friday nights?"

Ron asked, "What does that have to do with anything?"

Eric added, "We camped two Mondays and Tuesdays."

Junior spoke, "I believe they know when you camp."

Eric asked, "How would they know that?"

Ron added, "We camp early in the week and other times toward the end."

"Wait a minute," Eugene eagerly inserted into the conversation, "Didn't that girl that sat behind us on the bus call her dad 'George'? Doesn't she live south of the cave?"

Eric said, "So she could have heard us talking about camping and told her parents?"

"I believe you're right, and I know her parents." The bus driver was slow to speak, "To avoid you, the moonshiners ran their operation when they knew you were not camping, then stored it in glass jars along the path. Fellows, we need to cut this camping trip short and let the law handle this moonshine still; I know this Ellen and her husband, and they are bad characters."

The trio looked intently at each other, and finally, Eric spoke, "I suppose you're right, Junior. We are glad you came with us."

Junior thought for a minute and said, "You need what Proverbs 2:11 says: 'Discretion will protect you, and understanding will guard you,' so now you understand this could have been unsafe to continue around the moonshine still?"

Ron said, "We now see that this operation is large with at least five or more characters."

Then Eugene added, "Arthur and Allen sure looked rough, and I know my parents will appreciate your guidance."

Eric said, "Mine too, thanks, Junior."

"Boys before we go, I need to tell you something. Eric's mother overheard you three talking about the still and told your dad, then he asked me to come with you; fooling around with moonshiners can become dangerous. No hard feelings?"

The trio spoke in unison, "No hard feelings."

The foursome left for home anticipating another spelunking trip soon. The three seventeen-year-olds had gained wisdom, and the forty-year-old recaptured a little boyish fun. Age has little to do with a lasting friendship.

In late October, Arthur, George, and Allen were caught by the county sheriff with several jars of illegal moonshine and to reduce jail time, they led the authorities to the still. They destroyed it, and Ellen and her husband received a lengthy jail sentence; it would be safer now for the teenagers to explore the cave.

Julie enrolled in accounting classes at the local community college.

CHAPTER 16

ERIC'S JUNIOR AND SENIOR YEAR

(1958–1959) MR. BOB CONTINUED TO BE Eric's favorite teacher during his junior year; the explanation of geometry simplified algebra and trigonometry. It thrilled Eric to apply the knowledge of linear, circular, and three-dimensional measurements in the Industrial Arts Laboratory; he discovered many uses for inches, angles, degrees, radii, and diameters. Later in life, these interests and skills guided Eric's career choice.

Eric's grandfather's health continued to decline during Eric's junior year; eighteen-year-old Eric devoted additional time throughout the week to assist his ailing grandparents.

(1959-60) Eric, now a senior, anticipated the beginning of school in late August; it was a reprieve from another hard, hot, and sometimes dirty, smelly farm work. Fall work of gathering corn, making sorghum, stripping tobacco, and repairing fences required hours of hard work.

Eric anticipated bagging squirrels during hunting season in August for his parents and grandparents. Later in the fall, he would hunt rabbits for them. His grandfather was raised in the East Tennessee mountains and longed for this wild flavored dish. For the past several years, Eric had been able to fulfill these requests. Now, at the age of sixty-seven, his grandfather's health had begun to deteriorate, and in June, he was placed in the hospital for medical attention. Gangrene in his leg necessitated amputation at the knee. His out-of-state family and many in the local community visited him with wishes of regaining his health so he could return home.

Removal of his lower leg required an urgent blood transfusion; the hospital blood bank was low, and no adult present in the immediate family matched his blood type. It was not recommended for a young person of eighteen to give blood; however, Eric convinced the hospital staff that he wanted to help his beloved grandfather, so they should type his. It was acceptable, so his grandfather received lifeblood from his grandson.

The next day, Eric and his mother were sitting next to his grandfather's hospital bed when he looked at Eric and said, "You know son, God created man with two legs to walk around on this earth, and now I want to go home."

Eric glanced at his Mom's tear-stained face knowing that his papaw was not able to go home until his amputated leg healed. Eric would not have understood the true meaning of this statement when he was thirteen, nor did he understand it now at eighteen. His mother, with a distant look on her face, slowly shook her head. Later she explained that Papaw meant going home to Heaven; he convinced her that without one leg, he wanted to depart this life. Eric's grandfather enjoyed the smell of freshly disturbed earth in the garden and the "new ground" he cleared three times; it was his connection to God creating the earth and everything in it. This conversation between his grandfather, his mother, and himself would forever remain in his memory.

On the third day of his hospital stay, as Eric and his parents walked into the room, Papaw was enraged with two sons-in-law. A nurse had demanded he give her his little pocket knife; he refused. Others in the family tried unsuccessfully to convince him to hand over the knife, so the two sons-in-law insisted he give it to them. Their approach angered him so much he threatened them with an open blade. Eric's grandmother asked the nurses why he was so irate, and they told her it was probably his medications. After witnessing the situation for some time, Eric suggested everyone leave the room and let him speak to his grandfather.

"Papaw why did the nurse want that little knife?"

With a hoarse reply, he said, "I don't know. She just wanted it."

"Papaw, you don't want to hurt anyone, do you?"

"Of course not, son. I just use it to cut my chews," he explained.

The hospital permitted him to continue his habit of chewing tobacco while confined to his room if he could sit in a wheelchair. The physicians told the family that it would not do further harm to his present condition, so they allowed it; the nursing staff thought it was ridiculous and intended to override the doctor's consent.

After a gentle reminder of Papaw's blood transfusion, Eric asked for the knife, and it was given to him without hesitation.

"Papaw, I'll give Grandma the knife, and she can cut your chews for you, okay?"

The twenty-second day of June was a sad day for eighteen-year-old Eric; his affable and wise grandfather passed away. On the day of his funeral, the little country church overflowed with grieving relatives and neighbors; his grandchildren and the young people in the community numbered more than the adults. Eric would miss those thoughtful and engaging moments he had had with him, especially the ones explaining the biblical principles Eric had so often spoken to him about. Due to his gentle encouragement and guidance, Eric was able to release resentment and even anger at some unkind adult. His grandfather explained that Eric's struggles with his Christianity were common for young Christians.

Eric's life was about to change; now he had to study to understand God's messages to him. Even though Eric would graduate from high school in one year, he still took jaunts to his favorite woods. While sitting on the stump gazing into the azure sky through the leafy canopy, he would mull questions such as: *why did God take Papaw at the age of almost sixty-eight? Has he gone to Heaven? Is God telling me something about his death? Am I a good Christian? Did I understand enough about being baptized? Who can I talk to now? My parents, the preacher, a neighbor, or my very close friends, Ron, and Eugene?* This trio had spent hours roaming the countryside discussing the whys of many life activities.

In late August, Eric enrolled for his final year of high school. Miss Samantha had retired, and her replacement was Mr. Bob's wife. Eric's reputation as a lockpicker preceded him. She was as interested in the education of children as Miss Samantha. Eric was fond of their urging him in his reading adventures, from the exploits of outdoorsmen to world geography and everything in between.

After Christmas break, Eric was in Social Studies class, when someone knocked on the door. The teacher, Mr. Gene, had an urgent call in the office downstairs; it was necessary for him to answer it immediately. He instructed the class to continue reading and studying the assignment. Within minutes of his departure, books, shoes, and anything that was loose began to fly across the room. The only way Eric, Ron, and Eugene participated in the pandemonium was by ducking flying objects. Picking up the tennis shoe that had just hit him in the chest, Eric pulled it back to hurl it back across the room; at the height of his drawback, the door opened. Mr. Gene stood for a moment looking at the disorder on the floor, window seals, and on his desk.

With a frown and tight lips, he asked, "Okay, who threw? It looks like everyone was involved."

With all the complacent and smug faces, no one answered; "Eric, I know you're guilty because I saw you; go to the office."

Eric said, "But Mr. Gene, I didn't throw a thing."

"Why were you holding that shoe over your head, airing it out?"

"No sir, I haven't thrown a thing, but I would have. I was tired of dodging, and this hit me in the chest. About everyone was throwing books, shoes, or anything they could pick up," Eric reasoned with one of his favorite teachers.

"Go to the office anyway," he demanded. He did not inquire further or asked who took part in the mayhem.

Walking downstairs to the principal's office, Eric explained his recent intentions. Mr. Halbright cleared his throat and said, "Eric, since you have never been in my office, I'll tell you what I'm going to do. I'll let you pass on this one, and if you are ever sent to this office again, I'll double the punishment. You got that young man?"

Gratefully Eric answered, "Yes sir, thank you Mr. Halbright."

On the way across campus to the lunchroom, the trio was incredulous to the mendaciousness of the entire class. Feeling guilty that Eric was singled out, Eugene said, "I should have confessed and gone with you to the office."

"You didn't throw anything."

"No, but I picked up a shoe or two and pitched them to the floor."

"That is not the same as what I was going to do; if Mr. Gene had been a few seconds later, I would have thrown it and maybe hurt someone. Thanks, Eugene. I appreciate the thought."

Unknown to Eric or Eugene, Ron was silently observing the reactions of these Christians. *Do eighteen-year-old young people analyze responses to situations? Will he respond in the same way given the same circumstances? Is he spiritually mature enough to weigh the quality of this one incident in building one's character? Is his close friendship the same as his connection with his parents? Does he examine his parents' behavior as he does of this bonded duo?*

Later, the trio sat down to eat with Mr. Gene; he asked, "Eric, what did Mr. Halbright do?"

"He said he would let this one go, but if I'm ever sent to the office again, he will give me double punishment."

"You fellows know you are scheduled to take the aptitude test on Friday?"

Eugene asked, "Mr. Gene, how does this test help us and are we graded on it?"

"No, no grade, and it is designed to analyze your strengths and weaknesses."

Ron wanted in on the conversation, so he asks, "Does it quiz you on all your interests, your ability to solve problems, your temperament, your willingness to work, or effort. . ."

Mr. Gene answered, "Boy, Ron, you have a lot of questions. It is supposed to touch on all of these in some way, but I don't think it will assess effort."

Ron had more questions, "How about honesty, places to work. . .?"

As he got up from the table, Mr. Gene said, "This is a good test. You fellows will do well on it."

Eric asked, "Ron, have you taken a similar test before?"

"No, but Larry has, and he thought it did little to help him decide what career he chose."

Eight-forty Friday morning, the proctor seated the senior class for the lengthy exam. There were three exam sections: Math and Science, World Knowledge and Language Arts, and Dexterity and Aptitude. The Math and Science segment was the lengthiest, World Knowledge and Language next, and the shortest part was the individual Dexterity and Aptitude exam. After finishing the exam, on the way to the bus, they were eager to discuss some on the strange inquiries.

Junior announced with his usual toothy smile, "Come aboard."

Before the triad gathered on the seat directly behind Junior, discussion began on the validity of the Dexterity and Aptitude exam.

Eric asked, "Ron have you ever had a test like that one?" referring to the dexterity and aptitude part.

"Nope."

"Eugene, how about you?"

"Nope."

"Nope, me neither," came from the student yellow transport driver.

Ron said, "What are we going to do with him?"

Eugene said, "I know what we can do; the next time we take him camping, let's throw him into the swimming hole."

"Here, here," came from Ron and Eric.

Ron inquired, "Junior, are we teasing you too much?"

"No, not really. You know good-natured teasing is good if you care and respect the close friend you are joshing."

As Eric patted Junior on the back, he said, "Remember what it says in Job 12:12. 'Is not wisdom found among the aged?'"

"Here, here," came from Ron and Eugene.

"I'm not that old."

Eric said, "We know, but we still owe you for what you did to us in the cave and moving that hat to the moonshine still."

This reminder of the fun he had, produced a double-chuckle from Junior as he asked, "When can we go camping? I would like to do it soon because I know you will be finding work or going off to college and we won't have a chance to camp again."

Sunday morning, the teenagers sat in the little woodsided country church among a multitude of mixed parishioners: old, young, well-dressed, sleepy, those wanting to chitchat eager to hear the latest gossip, a serious deacon or two, Junior and Arlene Brooks, and the preacher, Mr. Huney. The service progressed as everyone was welcomed, announcements were made, three songs were sung, and then finally the sermon; "If Jesus came today, what would you say?" Mr. Hunley quoted several Scriptures, but when he referred to the Apostle Paul's longing to see the Thessalonians, one passage spoke to Eric, "Are not even ye in the presence of the Lord Jesus Christ at His coming?" 1 Thessalonians 2:19, (KJV)

Eric knew that when he accepted Christ at the age of thirteen, he repented, confessed, and was baptized for the forgiveness of his sins. He did it partially due to peer pressure, to please his parents, the congregation, and the minister. Toward the end of the sermon, he decided today he would do it for the right reason: to fully trust in the grace, mercy, love, hope, and the forgiving power of Jesus Christ. The sermon concluded, and the piano player began playing the song "I Am Thine O Lord."

> I am Thine, O Lord, I have heard Thy voice,
> And it told Thy love to me;
> But I long to rise in the arms of faith
> And be closer drawn to Thee.
> Draw me nearer, nearer blessed Lord,
> To the cross where Thou hast died.
> Draw me nearer, nearer, nearer blessed Lord,
> To Thy precious, bleeding side.

As the congregation finished the first chorus, Eric stepped into the aisle, walked to the minister, and said, "I now fully realized what becoming a Christian means. I know I must follow His commands, and I want to be baptized again." Before Eric sat down on the front seat, Ron had come to give his life to Christ. The minister talked to Ron then asked him to sit beside Eric; the congregation continued singing.

> Consecrate me now to Thy service, Lord,
> By the power of grace divine;
> Let my soul look up with a steadfast hope,
> And my will be lost in Thine.

The singing continued; Eugene came and hugged Ron, then sat between them.

> O the pure delight of a single hour
> That before Thy throne I spend,
> When I kneel in prayer, and with Thee, my God
> I commune as friend with friend!
> There are depths of love that I cannot know
> Till I cross the narrow sea;
> There are heights of joy that I may not reach
> Till I rest in peace with Thee.

After the service concluded, the two soon-to-be-high-school-graduates were baptized in Buck Creek. Everyone expressed happiness of Ron's decision and Eric's rededication. The preacher quoted Luke 15:10 (NIV): "In the same way, I tell you, there is rejoicing in the presence of the angels of God over one sinner who repents." He then dismissed the creek-side gathering with a prayer.

The last Friday of high school, the test proctor spoke to each teenager. He talked to Eric first; "Eric you did well in each section and scored high on the dexterity and aptitude test; do you have a question?"

"No," Eric answered. He thought, *why didn't he mention the other two exams? I know I did well on the math and geography.*

"What are your interests? Have you chosen a career? What do you want to do after you have graduated?"

"I haven't given it much thought," Eric answered. "I might learn how to repair clocks and watches."

"Well, I'm giving you advice on what the test suggested as a suitable career choice. With your background and size, you can be a successful farmer. If you have no questions, I'm through; you may leave."

Without another word, Eric, looking into the squinty eyes behind the thick spectacles, got up and left. When he met Ron in the hallway, Eric held up his hands and shrugged his shoulders; Ron smiled.

On the way home, Junior asked, "Can we camp this next week?"

"I can go."

"Me too," Ron answered.

Eric followed by saying, "I might be able to get away for a couple of days because Dad has cut back on the corn and tobacco acreage."

Junior eagerly added, "That sounds like fun; let me know when, okay?"

The following Thursday morning, the foursome met at the concrete culvert and slid over the grassy bank and continued downstream toward the waterfall and the cave system. Junior was eager to be with the teenagers; he led the way carrying his large backpack. When Ron inquired about the size of what he was toting, Junior said it was extra food. Knowing about his previous trickster behavior, the boys wondered what surprise he had brought to frighten them. Just after they passed the swimming hole, the trio realized what drove him to lead; dunking in a swimming hole was no fun. They stopped at the waterfall and sat on the two-foot high bank of the little plateau surrounded by southern white pine. They all stood as Junior unshouldered his load and began to remove waxed-paper-wrapped sandwiches on slices of homemade wheat bread. Next, he removed a half-gallon glass bottle of buttermilk made yesterday by his wife, Arlene. The trio just stood there watching the display; their skepticism vanished when he said, "I know how you fellows love buttermilk, so my wife sent you buttermilk and sandwiches." Holding both open palms toward the food, he added, "Help yourself."

Ron now understood why the backpack Junior was toting was so large.

Eric said, "Junior, you shouldn't have. . ."

Eugene added, "Thanks Junior and be sure to thank Arlene for us."

Ron was quick to fill his metal-folding drinking cup with the prized drink; then he began wolfing down a roast beef sandwich. Holding up both the buttermilk and the sandwich in his hands, he said, "Boy, thanks to Junior, this is ever so good."

Raising his eyebrows, Junior said, "'Ever so good'? What kind of talk is that?"

Eugene grabbed a cup of buttermilk, and a sandwich before he said, "Don't pay him any attention; he's from the north."

Junior said, "I thought he was from Kentucky."

As Eric swallowed his first bite, he said, "Way, way up north, Northern Kentucky."

This exchange triggered genuine laughter that continued for several minutes.

The group of four sat on the bank with feet hanging just above the bubbling brook enjoying the pulsation of the waterfall. Sometimes the incoming water gathered on the top stone covered with vines, mosses, and lichens, then released to tumble down the thirty-foot jagged cliff. First, there was a loud splash; then several rippling sounds as it spread across the waterfall before joining the waters of Barney Branch. The downward flow created a mist that rose through the vegetation clinging to the cliff and then it disappeared into the atmosphere near the top of the bank.

After he finished lunch, Junior asked, "Have you decided what you want to do?"

Eric said, "The proctor revealed that I might want to farm. I don't see how putting round pegs in round holes, square pegs in square holes gauged anything."

"I know," Ron said, "It helps you put a square fence post into a square hole or a round post in a round hole."

When the laughter subsided, Junior asked, "Do you want to farm?"

"I'm not sure. I would like to study and become a horologist."

Eugene said, "The proctor told me I would be a good welder, so he suggested I enroll in the vocational school."

Junior asked, "Do you want to weld?"

"No."

Junior asked, "Ron, what do you want to do?"

"My brother Larry encouraged me to apply to a bank or an accounting office for a job and then someday, study accounting."

"Fellows, I have known you for six years, and I have been and will continue praying that God will lead each of you as you travel through life." Revealing this, Junior raised his hands toward the heavens, saying, "Lord bless and guide these young men as they start life as young adults."

Taken aback by his comments and prayer, the trio remained silent for several minutes.

The small dark cloud unnoticed by the group slid low just over the treetops and started to drop its retained moisture quickly. No one had thought of bringing personal raingear, and the rainproof fabric was tied and concealed in Eric's backpack.

Ron said, "Let's go to the cave's overhang."

"Off in the rain we go," sang Eugene.

As they moved toward the cave's entrance, the group jumped across gravel bars, onto the bank, over fallen trees, and ran around thickets; they became drenched. The downpour stopped as suddenly as it had begun.

Ron asked, "How did we miss that raincloud?"

"I know," Eugene said, "Eric was so concerned about square and round pegs, we just didn't notice it until it was too late."

Eric smiled and said, "Instead of becoming a welder, maybe you should check into becoming a comedian."

Junior Brooks, the yellow student transport driver, understood this healthy joshing was preconditioning. It was a positive analytical critiquing of future efforts, whether it be about a comment on one's work or something one had written. While in the Army, he learned that criticism affected people two ways: those who thought it was belittling, regressed into self-pity, while others turned it into self-improvement. He found that a Christian man with the attitude of self-examination usually is a man who pleases God, and to that man, "God gives wisdom, knowledge, and happiness" Ecclesiastes 2:26, (NIV).

The foursome moved downstream to the cave and arranged the sleeping quarters under the rainproof fabric; Eugene and Ron on the south side of Junior, the bus driver, and Eric on the north.

"I have a long rope," Junior said as he pulled it from his backpack. "Let's remove our shirts and hang them on it; they will dry in a few minutes."

Ron grabbed the rope and tied it to a small oak tree; Junior took the other end, attached a rock to it and threw it over a tree limb about twelve feet above the campsite. When the stone brought the rope to the ground, he fastened the rope to the trunk loose enough to let the rope sag, so all shirts could be hung on it to dry.

Ron asked, "Why are you tying that end so high?"

"We might want to hang our food on it tonight; there are a lot of raccoons around here."

"Yes, I know. We see or hear them every time we camp."

Eric and Eugene were near the fire ring and didn't hear the comment about tying the rope. It took only a few minutes for the shirts to dry in the warm, gentle breeze. After the shirts dried, Junior tied the rope taut between the trees; one end of the rope was five feet above the sleeping bags, and the other end was tied twelve feet high.

The foursome was off to explore the cave. When they emerged, the sun was low in the western horizon, and a few rain-laden clouds drifted to the southeast. For supper, Junior's wife Arlene treated them with canned homemade beef-vegetable soup with cornbread. This action of Junior and his wife was a testament to their affection for the trio. They enjoyed popcorn and talked of many topics far into the night; they chatted about farm work, church, Christianity, teachers, girls, school, careers, moonshining, the cave, and the ghost of Mr. Culhwich.

About one o'clock in the morning, the group laid on their sleeping bags gazing at the moonlit low stratus clouds that had drifted southward by a gentle breeze. It was a pleasant evening that this group of four would long remember.

Eric turned and winked at Junior, then he said, "Junior this is the kind of night the Culhwich's ghost becomes the most active."

"That's right. I've heard older people say that when he is about to show himself, he starts singing."

Ron added, "I think I heard him the last time we camped."

"Me too," Eugene said.

Eric asked, "Did either of you see him?"

"Of course not," Ron answered.

Eugene smiled and said, "I think I saw something, it was kind of like a mist that fluttered about that tree."

Eric asked, "What tree?"

Pointing to the tree that Junior had tied the rope to earlier, he said, "That one."

Everyone laughed.

The conversation dwindled until Eugene began to snore; Eric had stopped talking; Ron's eyes slowly blinked, and Junior lay there with eyes wide open. Soon the teenagers were fast asleep; Junior was wide awake, enjoying the moment. The trio slept for fifteen minutes before Junior began creating the "Culhwich Ghost"; a white sheet hung on a four-foot long stick under a small pulley attached to the high rope. The southern breeze carried a soft moaning song across the campsite; it roused no one. Then there was a sob, no one moved, and finally, a high-pitched wail that echoed up and down Barney Branch, back and forth from the cliff to the timberline.

As Eric sprang to his feet, he grabbed his walking stick; Ron and Eugene leaped up with their walking sticks in hand as well. The trio stood with mouths open, eyes glaring, bended knees with both hands on their contorted walking sticks, ready to defend themselves against any intruder; now the ghost dove from the tree top fluttering straight toward them with arms flapping in the wind. As the "Culhwich Ghost" rushed toward his victims, Junior added screaming to the high-pitched wails.

As the ghost careened toward Ron, with glaring eyes, he swung his stick before it reached him; he missed; Eugene ducked, and the ghost engulfed Eric as he brandished his contorted sapling. By now, Junior grabbed his knees giggling and then in uncontrollable laughter. When the three racing hearts returned to normal, he had fallen to the ground, holding his sides, and guffawing like these teenagers had never seen or heard before. By the time the trio gathered themselves and walked over to him, his tear-stained face told everything. The three gathered around this fortysomething adult witnessing his hilarity; he laid beating the ground with his hands and laughing. When the laughter subsided to a giggle, he opened his eyes, and the look on their faces triggered another laughter episode. He had laughed so long and hard, the sound of his voice weakened into a snicker.

Ron, who stood there looking at Junior, said, "What are we going to do with him?"

Eugene spoke up and said, "We told him we were going to throw him in the swimming hole, but we can't carry him at night; it's too far."

Eric moved to the other side of the figure on the ground and said, "I don't believe Junior can get up so let's help him."

Junior said, "I've never had so much fun in my life." Then he followed it with a half-suppressed laugh.

Eric nodded toward Barney Branch as Ron and Eugene leaned down to help Junior to his feet. Both understood what the head nod meant. Ron and Eric grabbed Junior's arms while Eugene grabbed his feet and before Junior knew what was happening, he was on his way to the deepest part of the creek by the campsite. Too late to resist these strong farm teenagers, he politely laid in the water, with an occasional chuckle. The triad, after the initial fright, had as much fun as Junior. The group gathered around the sleeping bags; two dried their feet, one put on a pair of dry socks, and another had to dress entirely in dry clothing. This camping trip was etched into their memory forever. The need for a dunking was satisfied with the early morning soaking, so they passed the swimming hole on their way home.

What does it take for an older person to be compatible and influential in the lives of teenagers? Should the teenager reason like the adult or the adult think like the teenager? Are adults born with this gift? Is it learned, taught in Sunday School, or is it because of similar personalities? Did Junior's desire to protect them from the physical hurt of a malevolent moonshiner, or his trickster activities translate into "love thy brother"?

CHAPTER 17

AFTER HIGH SCHOOL GRADUATION

ON THE SIXTH OF JUNE 1960, ERIC'S sister and her husband took the nineteen-year-old Eric to Bradley University, in Peoria, Illinois, to register in the Horology Division.

Eric missed his friends back home, but soon developed a friendship with Ellis Duke from Southbend, Indiana and Rocky Ford of southern Arkansas. After the all-day class, they ate supper at a corner drugstore grill. When Becky, a forty-two-year-old waitress realized Eric was a Kentucky boy, she favored him with extra food. The preferential treatment he received was due to her perception of all Kentuckians. They were barefooted, poor, uneducated, untraveled homebodies. All houses were built on stilts, and the hollows were so deep that the sun shone only between ten in the morning and three in the afternoon. The atypical knowledge of

Kentuckians rendered her unable to accept Eric's revealing of the truth; his family built a new house on flat land; it had running water. The shoes he was wearing were not his first, mules and cows didn't have legs that was shorter on one side, so they could walk on the steep hills, and his family didn't make moonshine.

It was ironic since Becky had never been out of the state of Illinois, though Eric was not well-traveled, he had been in Ohio, Indiana, and now Illinois. She had no desire for any travel; Eric wanted to see the world, especially Alaska, Jerusalem, and Australia.

Eric had more money than he ever had before. He was confident that he had enough to pay his way through three sections of school until he graduated. He had a bulging pocket full of money, 928 dollars. The required costly equipment and tools soon lessened his resources. In a few short weeks, with Eric's interest in the art of timepieces and his applied skills, he successfully graduated in watch repair and watchmaking. Diamond cutting and stone setting were next; then a long apprenticeship under a master craftsman to become an expert in the art and science of time measurement, stone cutting, and polishing.

His overstuffed pocket soon became flat.

Nine o'clock Monday morning, with little money, one small suitcase, and a plastic bag full of his belongings, Eric began hitchhiking to Eubank, Kentucky. Four rides placed him in Frankfort, Kentucky as the sun disappeared in the western horizon. Eric sat on a bench one block away from the Greyhound Bus Station contemplating what to do. Darkness would hamper drivers seeing him, and fewer would be on the highways. He walked to the bus station, and asked, "Sir, how much is a ticket to Eubank, Kentucky?"

The ticket agent said, "Five dollars and fifty-five cents. The bus leaves in thirty minutes."

Eric walked back to the bench under the dim streetlamp to count his money. The total of his cash was three dollars and eighty-five cents. He was alone in the darkness, weary, hungry, with no friends, little money, and a squashed spirit. He thought, *I wish I could talk to someone.* Knowing he had not attended church or prayed while in Illinois, he wondered if God would listen. Bowing his head, he prayed, "Lord, forgive me for not talking to you while I've been away from home, but Lord, what should I do? I'm a dollar and seventy cents short? Should I stay in the station and hitchhike tomorrow?" He waited for an answer, none came. Walking back to the station he selected a corner bench; on the far side, two intoxicated men lay snoring. Lonesome thoughts flashed across his mind. *I wish I had a bowl of Mom's homemade vegetable soup, a slab of cornbread, and a big glass of buttermilk. Home would be pleasant and safe.* Another thought trickled across his consciousness, *my billfold,* he thought; *those intoxicated men might demand my wallet, but why would they want it? It's empty.* Suddenly, Eric remembered, his dad had given him a two-dollar bill to put in the wallet picture window as a good luck omen. He quickly removed the money, dashed to the ticket window, and purchased a pass to Eubank.

Eric grabbed his small tattered suitcase, the plastic bag, and rushed to the loading platform just as a bus drove up. A well-dressed uniformed Greyhound bus driver stood up and announced, "The restrooms are inside. We leave in five minutes for all points south: Lawrenceburg, Harrodsburg, Danville, Stanford, Eubank, Somerset, and every burg in between."

Three people followed the driver down the steps and went inside.

Pointing to the door, he added, "You may board anytime."

When Eric entered with both pieces of his luggage, only two seats were empty. As he slid his belongings under the seat, one of the intoxicated men horizontally occupied the empty seat directly across the aisle; then he fell asleep. The second drunk sat down with Eric and Eric was trapped against the window. The drunk's body odor was unbearable; Eric could have survived a whiff, but he was inundated with the appalling stink; it shrouded him like a dense smoke or thick fog. Eric tried holding his breath, but after two minutes, he realized breathing was essential for him to stay alive. The smell would probably not kill him.

Ten miles down the road, the bus stopped at an intersection; two riders exited to a waiting car. Filled with ecstasy, he saw the vacancy, an empty seat. *I must hastily move to that empty seat,* he thought. Eric developed a secret plan. It would take hours to reach Eubank because the bus stopped briefly in every community, and in larger towns, it delayed its departure to the announced time. Eric had to move.

"Excuse me," Eric said as he stood up, "I'm going to that empty seat."

The drunk turned his wobbly head and said, slurring through cracked lips, "You can't move, son; if you do, I won't have any friends."

"I know, but you look tired, and you need to lie down."

"You are right, right. What did you say about sleeping?" he asked. "Okay buddy, you be careful now, won't you son?"

Eric slipped past his knees as the intoxicated man waved a shaky finger toward the empty seat.

At two twenty-five AM, Eric started the eight-mile walk home, carrying his frayed suitcase and a plastic bag; he hoped to eat breakfast at home. After two miles of lugging his heavy belongings, he stopped to rest. As he sat on the bank, the billfold crossed his mind again. *Have I lost it or did that man steal it?* Eric made sure it was in his pocket. He thought, *why would anyone want to take it? The only worthwhile things in it are my driver's license and a picture of Mom and Dad. There are no money or credit cards.* He sat there mulling about his long day, then he dropped his head and prayed, "Lord, thank you for telling me about the two-dollar bill I had in my billfold and delivering me from those stoned dudes. Lord, I know Job spoke to you 'in the anguish of his spirit to complain in the bitterness of his soul' because his misfortunes were so great. I have not lost my family, and the only hardships I had were being lonely, afraid, hungry, and weak; please Lord, forgive me."

The big full moon appeared brighter as a rain cloud drifted to the east. Eric grasped his suitcase and a plastic bag, jumped into the road, and started the six-mile walk. About a mile along the road, Eric heard the whine of a motor as a vehicle accelerated onto Highway 70; then it changed to humming on its way toward Eric, who had moved to the grass shoulder.

The bright taillights illuminated as the pickup passed Eric; it stopped, backed up, and lowered the passenger's window, and a recognizable voice said, "Eric, want a ride home? What in the world are doing hitchhiking at three-thirty in the morning?"

Another drunk, but Eric knew this one. Eric thought, *"Lord, are you telling me that I should not be afraid of all drunks?"* He continued his thoughts, *if Hobert can keep this old rusty pickup in the road, it will be better than walking.* Eric threw his bags in the truck bed and climbed into the cab that smelled of a repulsive strong drink.

It was too early for his parents to be awake, so Eric decided to wait on the front porch. Whether it was a hunch, instinct, intuition, or a sixth sense, the door opened, and Mom said, "Eric, what are you doing here? Come on in, and I'll have breakfast in a few minutes."

Oh, those words are so beautiful, his soul was touched; it lingered as he walked inside and sat in the kitchen watching his mother cook. *I miss Mom's breakfast so much,* thought Eric. Did he overlook other emotions?

Eric's dad was still asleep.

Eric planned to find work and save enough money and return to Bradley University to finish his schooling. He found a job at a JJ Newberry's Five and Dime store in Frankfort for the next eighteen months as an assistant manager in training. Eric had been taught honesty, respect, dependability, and to work hard. He moved quickly through the classifications of a general laborer, supervisor of the stockroom, displaying and pricing merchandise on a long counter, to the final position of control over seventeen departments in ordering, pricing, presenting, and supervising one-third of the store employees.

Eric remembered the last day of his employment with the Newberry Company; it was break time on a Thursday afternoon, at about two PM. Mr. Hick, the store manager, was sitting at the lunch counter drinking coffee. Eric ordered coffee and sat on the next stool. They talked for five minutes about store troubles when Eric used the term, "I think," and Mr. Hick turned and angrily said, "Bray, I'm not paying you to think. I'm paying you for your back."

Another big truck ran over him; the truck hurt him now at the age of twenty-one as it did when he was four, five, seven, thirteen, and eighteen. Here came the method of handling those youthful jabs; to be silent, miserable, thoughts of *maybe I shouldn't have,* and isolation. At eight PM, Eric closed the store. He then collected his pay through that day, thanked the employees for their help and friendship, then he laid the ring of keys on his boss' desk and left.

Eric's little 1952 black Chevrolet coupe sat in his parents' driveway at 11 PM. Eric is twenty-one, two years post high school graduation, and still afflicted with the memory of early childhood jabs; what is he to do? Can Eric decide why he had so many distressing thoughts? Was it:

1. Being born into a poor farming family?

2. Not being able to talk plain when in elementary school?

3. Being made fun of by adults?

4. Regular church attendance?

5. Strict but loving parents?

6. Trusting and close friends?

7. Love and guidance of grandparents?

8. Patience of the Holy Spirit?

9. Forbearance of God?

What do you think? Did you have childhood problems? Have you told anyone about them? It is therapeutic to discuss what troubles you. Could it be that all children have similar difficulties in life?

A LITTLE ABOUT THE AUTHOR

WINSTON FLOYD OSBORNE was born February 3, 1941, to Eugene and Audrey Osborne. He has one sister and three brothers living and one sister deceased.

Graduating from Eubank High School in 1960, he attended Bradley University in Peoria, Illinois for a short study in the horology division (the art or skill of making clocks).

He graduated from Eastern Kentucky University in 1966 with a Bachelor of Science Degree in Industrial Arts/Education. He received his Master's Degree in 1968 with a Principal certification. His certification of Superintendence came after the sixth year of school.

He worked for the State Health Department for one and a half years, taught for five years, and was a principal for seventeen. He worked at the Pulaski County School System as Director of Transportation, Director of Finance, and three-and-a-half years as Assistant Superintendent, then retired in 1995.

He has taught youth to senior classes in his church.

He was his church's representative to a local, regional Bible camp for over twenty years and served as chairperson for two. He has been a deacon and an elder in the church for many years.

ACKNOWLEDGMENTS

ERIC'S REAL-LIFE BROTHER, PAUL, A Berea College graduate, encouraged him to try college for at least one year. It was the second-best decision Eric had made; the acceptance of Jesus Christ was the best. Eric's decision to attend college was supported by his entire family: his parents Eugene and Audrey, brother Charles, sisters Fern and Eleanor, and brother Darrell. Eric met his wife, Marlene Wesley, a Casey County native, and God blessed the union with a son, Brian, and a daughter, Margena; he now has three beautiful grandchildren.

Eugene West became a Methodist minister in Northern Kentucky, and Ron is a supervisor in a large factory in Ohio.

Many of the elderly friends in Eric's young life have since passed away, leaving a vastness of cherished memories.

Thanks to Marlene, my wife of fifty years, for the second pair of eyes to help edit this narrative.

Thanks to my Salem Author Center team for their help, patience, and guidance in this endeavor.

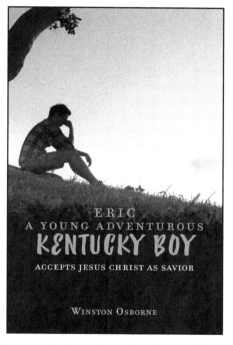

This is a sequel to Winston's first book, "Eric, A Young Adventurous KENTUCKY BOY."

CPSIA information can be obtained
at www.ICGtesting.com
Printed in the USA
FSHW021136080719
59791FS

9 781545 659915